# Advances in Data Science and Computing Technologies

# Advances in Applied Science and Engineering

# Advances in Data Science and Computing Technologies

**Machine Learning Algorithms for Engineering Applications: Future Trends and Research Directions**
Prasenjit Chatterjee, PhD (Editor)
Parmanand Astya, PhD (Editor)
Sudeshna Chakraborty, PhD (Editor)
Dr. Pooja (Editor)
2022. ISBN: 978-1-68507-449-4 (Hardcover)
2022. ISBN: 979-8-88697-086-9 (eBook)


More information about this series can be found at
https://novapublishers.com/product-category/series/advances-in-data-science-and-computing-technologies-edited-series/


# Advances in Applied Science and Engineering

**Understanding Information Entropy**
Vijay Kumar, PhD (Editor)
2023. ISBN: 979-8-88697-839-1 (Hardcover)
2023. ISBN: 979-8-88697-894-0 (eBook)

**Situational Modeling: Definitions, Awareness, Simulation**
Alexander Fridman, PhD (Editor)
2023. ISBN: 979-8-88697-590-1 (Hardcover)
2023. ISBN: 979-8-88697-725-7 (eBook)


More information about this series can be found at
https://novapublishers.com/product-category/series/advances-in-applied-science-and-engineering/

Kavita Saini
Amar Kumar
and J. N. Singh
Editors

# Blockchain and EHR

**Copyright © 2024 by Nova Science Publishers, Inc.**

**All rights reserved.** No part of this book may be reproduced, stored in a retrieval system or transmitted in any form or by any means: electronic, electrostatic, magnetic, tape, mechanical photocopying, recording or otherwise without the written permission of the Publisher.

We have partnered with Copyright Clearance Center to make it easy for you to obtain permissions to reuse content from this publication. Please visit copyright.com and search by Title, ISBN, or ISSN.

For further questions about using the service on copyright.com, please contact:

|  | Copyright Clearance Center |  |
|---|---|---|
| Phone: +1-(978) 750-8400 | Fax: +1-(978) 750-4470 | E-mail: info@copyright.com |

## NOTICE TO THE READER

The Publisher has taken reasonable care in the preparation of this book but makes no expressed or implied warranty of any kind and assumes no responsibility for any errors or omissions. No liability is assumed for incidental or consequential damages in connection with or arising out of information contained in this book. The Publisher shall not be liable for any special, consequential, or exemplary damages resulting, in whole or in part, from the readers' use of, or reliance upon, this material. Any parts of this book based on government reports are so indicated and copyright is claimed for those parts to the extent applicable to compilations of such works.

Independent verification should be sought for any data, advice or recommendations contained in this book. In addition, no responsibility is assumed by the Publisher for any injury and/or damage to persons or property arising from any methods, products, instructions, ideas or otherwise contained in this publication.

This publication is designed to provide accurate and authoritative information with regards to the subject matter covered herein. It is sold with the clear understanding that the Publisher is not engaged in rendering legal or any other professional services. If legal or any other expert assistance is required, the services of a competent person should be sought. FROM A DECLARATION OF PARTICIPANTS JOINTLY ADOPTED BY A COMMITTEE OF THE AMERICAN BAR ASSOCIATION AND A COMMITTEE OF PUBLISHERS.

## Library of Congress Cataloging-in-Publication Data

Names: Saini, Kavita, 1976- editor.
Title: Blockchain and EHR / editors Kavita Saini, PhD, School of Computing Science and Engineering, Galgotias University, Delhi NCR, India, Amar Kumar, general manager, HCL Technologies Ltd. India, J.N. Singh, PhD, Designation: Professor, SCSE, Galgotias University, Greater Noida, India.
Identifiers: LCCN 2024003160 (print) | LCCN 2024003161 (ebook) | ISBN
  9798891133808 (paperback) | ISBN 9798891135543 (adobe pdf)
Subjects: LCSH: Information storage and retrieval systems--Medical records.
  | Blockchains (Databases) | Medical records--Data processing--Management. | Medical records--Data processing--Security measures.
Classification: LCC R864 .B56 2024 (print) | LCC R864 (ebook) | DDC
  651.5/04261--dc23/eng/20240228
LC record available at https://lccn.loc.gov/2024003160
LC ebook record available at https://lccn.loc.gov/2024003161

# Published by Nova Science Publishers, Inc. † New York

# Contents

| | | |
|---|---|---|
| **Preface** | | vii |
| **Chapter 1** | **A Review of Applications and Security: Blockchain Technology** ...... 1 |
| | Mohsin Imam and Kavita Saini | |
| **Chapter 2** | **An Extensive Study of Blockchain Technology: Privacy Perspective** ...... 21 |
| | Brijesh Kumar Bhardwaj, Kavita Srivastava, Anshul Mishra and J. N. Singh | |
| **Chapter 3** | **Proposed Evaluation Framework for Blockchain Technology** ...... 33 |
| | Brijesh Kumar Bhardwaj, Kavita Srivastava, Neeraj Kumar Tiwari and J. N. Singh | |
| **Chapter 4** | **Online Voting System on a Secure Platform - Blockchain** ...... 45 |
| | Bankuri Singhal, Mahesh Kuma, Poras Khaterpal, Prakhar Priyadarshi and Mohit Dayal | |
| **Chapter 5** | **Enhancing Data Storage Security Using Web3 and Cryptography** ...... 59 |
| | Bishal Kumar, Janhavi Soni, Sudeep Singh Yadav and J. N. Singh | |
| **Chapter 6** | **Securing Electronic Healthcare Records Using Blockchain: Is It a Viable Solution** ...... 89 |
| | Pooja Saigal | |

| Chapter 7 | Token Generation Using Blockchain Technology ................................................109 |
|---|---|
| | Mahesh Kumar, Poras Khaterpal, Rohit Kumar Mahato, Ayush Kumar and Mohit Dayal |

**About the Editors**....................................................................................121
**Index** ...................................................................................125

# Preface

Blockchain is a decentralized transaction and information control generation advanced first for Bitcoin cryptocurrency. Since blockchain no longer has a centralized substance, the trade statistics are disseminated in a decentralized peer-to-peer setting to induce confirmation. There are many Key Characteristics of Blockchain Technology such as Decentralization, Reliability, tamper proof and Transparency.

The book is divided in eight chapters and explain the blockchain technology and its applications in healthcare industries in detail.

The blockchain technology offers a variety of alternatives for various types of infrastructure and has huge potential for a wide range of applications. Blockchain technology is based on distributed and secure decentralized protocols. There is no central authority or point of control, and the network's nodes themselves generate, add, and validate the data blocks.

Chapter 1 discusses about transaction security through blockchain technology. Every transaction is recorded in a block, which will behave as a record book and help in maintaining transparency and security.

Henceforth, this part investigated and broke down blockchain framework security episodes to comprehend blockchain framework with hash, blockchain, and conveyed framework, as well as to give a security assessment structure to blockchain frameworks.

Chapter 2 talks about Smart Contract, Hash Function, Blockchain Evaluation with Hash Function, Coinbase Transaction Structure in detail.

Blockchain technology advances secure figuring without experts in an open architecture. Blockchain technology is utilised in bit currency transactions, information sharing, record keeping, and other applications. Blockchain link blocks using hash codes from a hash function. Chapter 3 explains the cryptic situation of blockchain-based applications across various regions. The reason for it is to investigate the current status of blockchain advancement and its crypto applications.

At last, another investigation of a blockchain-based cryptography stage is introduced tending to the flow hash plans, trailed by suggestions for future blockchain analysts and engineers. The presented chapter discusses about the evaluation for blockchain technology.

There are several serious problems with the present traditional voting procedures, such as a lack of security and transparency. A distributed ledger can be used to build an easy-to-use and reliable system for handling and storing any digital data.

The switch to electronic voting allowed for a reduction in the expenditures associated with planning and conducting elections, but the security of this procedure is still an unresolved question. Chapter 4 talks about the electronic voting system which provides the high security offered through the blockchain technology.

In IoT the involvement of blockchain is to get a methodology for processing existing data by smart objects. In order to guarantee interaction between network nodes, the Internet of Things requires such innovations in a centralized environment. Chapter 5 looked at this approach, its advantages, and its obstacles involved.

Web applications have been governed by centralized providers for a significant portion of the history of the Internet. The logic and data of the program are controlled by these suppliers, who have complete control over editing and erasing it.

Chapter 6 talks about WEB3.0, which uses blockchain as a medium to work, reducing the factor of data loss or leaks, as blockchain is fundamentally unalterable making them more secure for data storage. Blockchain is a decentralized cloud storage system that ensures data security. Any computing node connected to the internet can join and form peer's network thereby maximizing resource utilization.

Electronic Healthcare Records (EHRs) are essential sources of highly private information that must routinely be exchanged across peers in the healthcare industry, to enable comprehensive data analysis and deliver individualised healthcare. The sharing of EHRs is hampered by the healthcare companies' cyberinfrastructure boundaries and potential privacy leaks. Chapter 7 presents the views on healthcare data management based on blockchain technology and prospective study areas for exchanging medical data via blockchain.

Token generation using blockchain technology is a revolutionary concept that leverages the power of distributed ledger systems to create digital tokens with various applications. These tokens are unique digital assets that, thanks to cryptographic principles, can stand for value, ownership, or even access privileges. Chapter 8 explains the procedure to generate token through step-by-step procedure.

Chapter 1

# A Review of Applications and Security: Blockchain Technology

**Mohsin Imam**[1,*]
**and Kavita Saini**[2,†]

[1]Department of Computer Science, Atma Ram Sanatan Dharma College, University of Delhi, India
[2]School of Computer Science and Engineering, Galgotias University, Delhi NCR, India

## Abstract

The evolution of industry has been significantly influenced by blockchain technology. Regarding security, data access, auditing, and transaction management inside digital platforms, blockchain decentralized technology and privacy protocols offer potential benefits to many businesses. Blockchain is based on distributed and secure decentralized protocols; there is no central authority or point of control, and the network's nodes generate, add, and validate the data blocks. Blockchains enable transparency by allowing each participant to observe transactions at any moment and smart contracts provide secure transactions, reducing the risk of third-party disruption. Ethereum is a decentralized platform that facilitates the execution of smart contracts. This allows developers to design markets that move funds in accordance with instructions issued years ago. Decentralization and immutability are the principal characteristics of blockchain and promote faster transactions and validation. The security and applications of blockchain technology can be reviewed and improved further. These security concerns ought to have an impact on transactions and offer some

---

[*] Corresponding Author's Email: mohsinimam651@gmail.com.
[†] Corresponding Author's Email: kavitasaini_2000@yahoo.com.

In: Blockchain and EHR
Editors: Kavita Saini, Amar Kumar and J. N. Singh
ISBN: 979-8-89113-380-8
© 2024 Nova Science Publishers, Inc.

protection against certain attacks and provide some solutions to these problems.

**Keywords**: blockchain, security, smart contracts, decentralization, Ethereum

## Introduction

The blockchain technology offers a variety of alternatives for various types of infrastructure and has huge potential for a wide range of applications [1]. Resource management is encouraged by technology, which also guarantees effective and secure communication. When parties perform financial transactions using Blockchain, trust is raised since it decreases the possibility of fraud and automatically generates a record of activity [2, 3]. Creating an automated background check for any system member. Because of its decentralized nature, Blockchain offers dependability and lowers the danger of entering a business arrangement with an unknown person.

Today, everyone uses advanced technology to communicate via the internet. Voice calls, video calls, messages, and images are all transmitted straight from sender to receiver via the internet. For this transaction, a trusted third party must be maintained between the sender and the receiver. In the old system, when it comes to money transactions, consumers must rely on a third party to execute them. Blockchain, on the other hand, will offer total transaction security [4]. Every transaction should be recorded in a block, which will act as a record book. A block is added to the blockchain as a permanent database whenever a transaction is complete [5, 6]. When a block is complete, a new block is either created or inserted, and each block stores the previous block's hash.

## Key Characteristics of Blockchain Technology

### Decentralization

The idea of decentralization is not revolutionary. Three network designs are frequently considered while creating technical solutions: centralized, distributed, and decentralized (Figure 1). Although decentralized networks are widely used by blockchain technology, a blockchain application cannot be purely categorized as decentralized or not. Decentralization is the process of moving control and decision-making from a centralized association (a person, business, server, or group of people) to a distributed network. Decentralized networks attempt to reduce the level of trust that members should have in one another and discourage them from exercising power or command over one another in a way that corrupts the network's potency [7]. Peer-to-peer networks, upon which blockchain networks are built, are also a decentralized type of network.

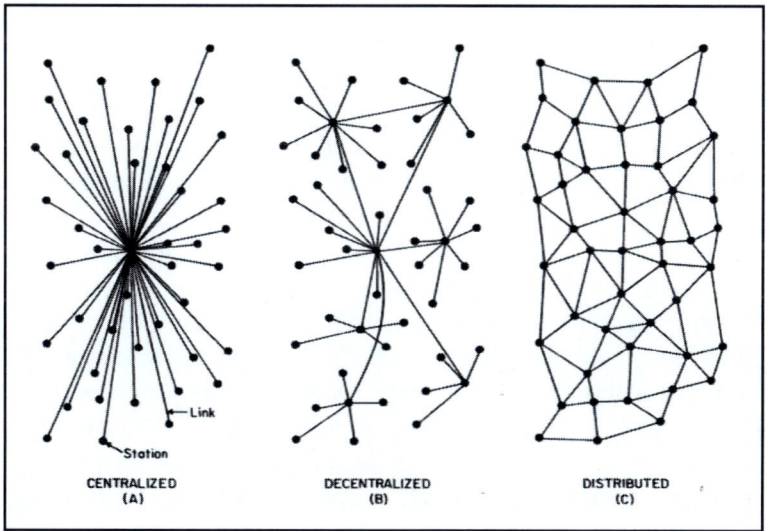

**Figure 1.** Architecture Comparison of Various Network.

Decentralization assures that the blockchain is not regulated by a single person, organization, or even the government. It is spread through a methodical digital network, preventing tampering with the transactions [8-10]. It offers greater security and flexibility than centralized applications. Because quick decision making is necessary, many organizations have opted for decentralization. Everything is done in the same spot in a centralized atmosphere. Where a decentralized environment operates in multiple locations.

## Reliability

Each block in Blockchain contains information about the previous block. During the transaction, it will give an authentication mechanism and no communication is done with the third party. Instead, a public ledger will be used. All transactions are logged in automatically within this ledger.

## Transparency

One of the major problems in the current industry is transparency. Organizations have attempted to impose more rules and regulations to increase openness [11]. However, there is one factor centralization that prevents any system from being completely transparent.

With blockchain, a company may create a fully decentralized network with no requirement for a centralized authority, increasing the transparency of the system. Peers execute transactions and validate them on a blockchain, which is made up of peers. While not all peers participate in the consensus technique, they can decide whether to take part in the validation process. The consensus approach is employed to give validation through decentralization [12, 13]. Each node stores a copy of the transaction record after it has been verified. The blockchain network manages transparency in this manner [13]. Transparency is just one of the many advantages that blockchain technology may provide to security companies, common end users, and even governments in the cybersecurity industry [14]. The header of each block in the blockchain contains a hash that is created using the SHA-256 cryptographic hash algorithm and that hash in the block header of each block also serves as a reference to a preceding block, also referred to as the parent block as illustrated in Figure 2 below.

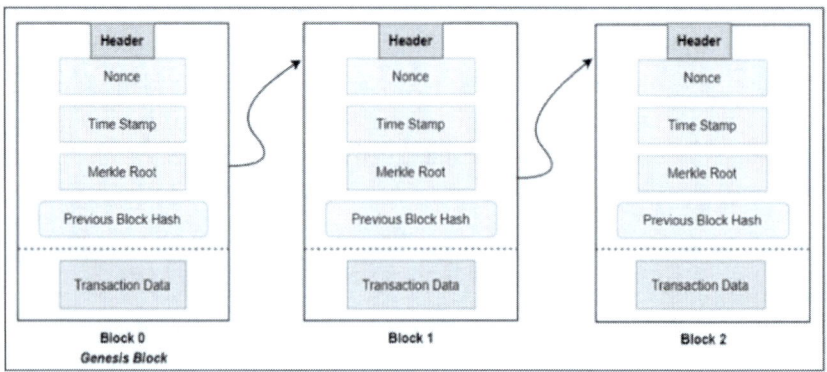

**Figure 2**. Structure of blocks in a Blockchain.

## No Intermediaries

In the Blockchain network, all transactions are peer-to-peer (P2P), eliminating the need for middlemen like banks, notaries, or governments. Business operations can be made highly automated by doing away with trust-establishing middlemen, which saves time and money. With automated supply chains and logistics, blockchain technology offers a lot of potential. Additionally, this characteristic reduces the possibility of financial fraud by centralized financial institutions like banks [15].

## Public and Private Blockchains

Blockchain is classified into three categories (Table 1). Blockchains might be public, private, or consortium based. This research focuses on a comparison of recent properties between public and private Blockchains. In terms of functionality, public and private blockchain should have many parallels as well as differences [16].

**Table 1.** Public vs Private Blockchain

| Public Blockchain | Private Blockchain |
| --- | --- |
| Large energy consumption | Low energy consumption |
| Open, anyone can join the network | Only certain, allowed nodes can join the network |
| Low transaction completion speed | Fast transaction completion speed |
| A high frequency of transaction approvals | A low frequency of transaction approvals |
| High transactional costs | Cost effective |
| Fully Decentralized | Semi Decentralized |
| Requires not trust among the node in the network | Nodes or Member need to trust each other in the network |

## Public Blockchain

Public Blockchains, sometimes referred to as permission-less blockchains, are totally transparent and adhere to the decentralization principle. Public Blockchains include things like Bitcoin and Ethereum. Anyone with access to the network can contribute blocks to the chain. In contrast to private blockchains, where the identities of the parties engaged in the transaction are kept secret, public blockchains are likewise mostly anonymous. The benefits of public blockchain include security, transparency, and anonymity; however, it appears that some drawbacks include high power consumption and scalability.

A public blockchain can be used to construct a completely open blockchain that is similar to Bitcoin and allows anybody to join and contribute to the network [17-20]. Anyone is ready to participate and take part in the essential operations of a public blockchain. A private blockchain owner or lead must issue an invitation or authorization before participants may participate. Enabling anybody to access, publish, and audit the most recent activity on the network, a public blockchain retains its self-governed nature. The infrastructure of the public blockchain network is totally decentralized. As a result, each node in the system will have a unique copy of the ledger. Additionally, they may efficiently update the ledger by employing consensus techniques.

**Private Blockchain**

A private blockchain network needs to be invited, and it must be approved by the network creator or by a set of regulations they've established. Companies that create private blockchains typically create a permissioned network. This limits who is permitted to use the network, and just for specific kinds of transactions. To participate, participants must get an invitation or authorization. A regulatory body could grant licenses for participation, a consortium could make the decisions, or current participants could choose future entrants as the access control mechanism. Once an organization joins the network, it will contribute to the decentralized upkeep of the blockchain.

One of the Hyperledger projects hosted by The Linux Foundation, Hyperledger Fabric is an illustration of a permissioned blockchain framework implementation. It was created from the ground up to meet these business needs. With this permissioned blockchain approach, enormous advantages can be realized by utilizing more than 30 years' worth of technical literature. Digital identification in particular is essential for the majority of industry use cases, whether they include resolving supply chain issues, upending the banking sector, or enabling secure patient/provider data exchanges in the healthcare sector. Only the parties involved in a given transaction will be aware of it and be able to access it; other parties will not be able to access it.

## Challenges with Blockchain Technology Implementations

Industry-wide, blockchain has encountered some difficulties, particularly during bitcoin transactions and recent attacks on different cryptocurrencies and DeFi chains. The fundamental issues listed below and depicted in Figure 3. Below is a list of some common difficulties [21] and.

### Scalability

Transactions are increasing everyday which may bring the scalability issue. Most businesses are suggesting the use of blockchain for their transactional procedures. Every transaction should be recorded and verified. The block's capacity will be extremely limited. Due to miners' preference for transactions with large transaction fees, some transactions must be delayed. Therefore, a large block size will slow down transaction speed, as a result scalability is a complex issue. Some solutions to the blockchain scalability issue include:

- Blockchain Storage Optimization
- Redesigning the Blockchain.

### Privacy

Users thought that while handling sensitive data, blockchain offers better privacy. Users on the blockchain could not generate their identities, only addresses. In 2013 Meiklejohn and in 2016 Kosba's research demonstrated that blockchain technology cannot ensure global privacy. According to a recent study, bitcoin transactions are connected to an account address in order to identify the user. The issues were identity leaks from users.

ECDHM, or elliptic curve Diffie-Hellman-Merkle, can be utilized to solve this issue. Both public and private keys will be addressed. It will assist in securing online message transactions. To maintain safe transactions, a secure platform like smart contracts and Ethereum is also being created.

### MITM Attack

Man in The Middle Attack is referred to as MITM [22, 23]. Here, a user may enter as an intermediary and may have been using a fake public key. He can quickly decode the sensitive data using this key. The participating nodes in blockchain share the public key. Each block needs a link to the one before it and the one after it. As a result, the public key is unchangeable and cannot be attacked by any forged keys.

**High Cost**

Blockchain is typically used to cut costs associated with third parties and intermediaries involved in the value transfer process. Although blockchain technology has many advantages, it is still in its infancy and hence difficult to integrate with existing systems. It makes it more expensive overall, deterring both the government and commercial companies from adopting it.

**DDoS Attack**

The big threat to blockchain is transaction flooding and brings the focus of DDoS attacks on the protocol layer of a blockchain. Attackers can work within the blockchain ecosystem to conduct a DDoS assault, or they can use traditional DDoS attacks on a blockchain to slow down its operations. Distributed Denial of Service (DDoS) attacks are directed at a single system, such as a computer, website, server, or other network resource [24]. As a result, the target system's connection or incoming messages may become sluggish, stop working altogether, or even crash. Particularly in the blockchain industry, DDoS attacks pose a significant business risk. Practically, it is impossible to stop this kind of attack.

Apart from the above-mentioned problems in blockchain, there are many other challenges as well for which companies and researchers are working on it to find its solution. In addition to the issues already highlighted, there are numerous additional issues with blockchain for which businesses and researchers are attempting to develop solutions. A few of the additional major challenges are depicted in Figure 3.

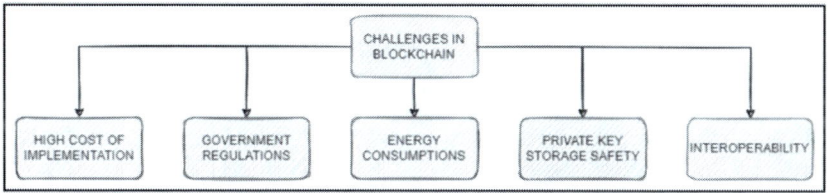

**Figure 3**. Challenges in Blockchain for Individuals and Businesses.

DDoS attacks aim to suspend the target services and make them unavailable to users. In a recent attack on GitHub, it is stated that "nearly a thousand separate autonomous systems spanning millions of unique endpoints" were responsible for the traffic. DDoS attacks typically come in a variety of forms, each of which uses a unique protocol and a botnet to carry out the attack. As a result, it will be exceedingly challenging for businesses to handle these attacks and rely on third parties to protect them against DDoS attacks [25].

## Cryptocurrency Attacks

Blockchain is the term for the technology that enables cryptocurrency (among other things). Blockchain technology was developed for the most well-known cryptocurrency, which is known as Bitcoin. Although, in recent years, blockchain has been built for more than only the transfer of digital monetary flow but major chunk of blockchain applications is covered by cryptocurrencies. Attacks against various cryptocurrencies have increased exponentially along with the growth in digital currency acceptance (Figure 4). One of the main ways to impair the cryptocurrency network is through a distributed denial-of-service (DDoS) attack. A malicious party can make a website or service unavailable by overloading a target with fictitious traffic. Cryptocurrencies are a prominent target for assault because to their prominence and value. The number of cryptocurrencies taken from various attacks from 2016 to 2020 is shown in Figure 4 below. This illustrates the sheer vulnerability of the Blockchain networks upon which these currencies are made upon, and how much work needs to be done to make these decentralized networks safer.

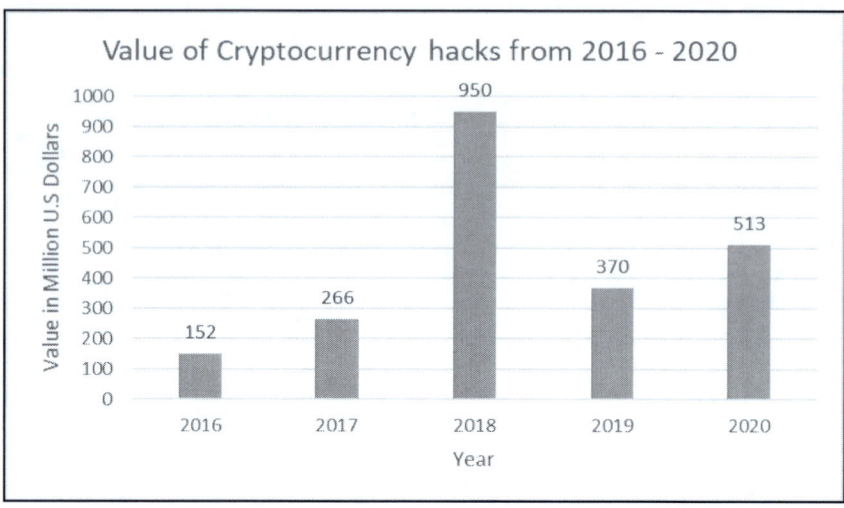

**Figure 4.** Value of Cryptocurrency Hacks Worldwide (2016 - 2020). Security Characteristics of Blockchain.

## Blockchain Ledger

The use of blockchain technology is decentralized. It will primarily facilitate peer-to-peer communication. Therefore, a network node is regarded as a computer. The distributed ledger copy should be available to these thousands of nodes. The transaction should be authenticated using this. A transaction cannot be carried out if any of the nodes are not in agreement with it. It will therefore be cancelled [26]. This will safeguard against a fraudulent transaction. Public ledgers make details of transactions and participants available to the public. Unlike private or federated ledgers, which can also be linked into a blockchain system, these ledgers lack security or authority. This is so that all other system users can maintain the network's ledger. To ensure a better result, this divided processing power among the computers.

Anyone with the necessary access can view the distributed ledger, which increases the process's transparency and dependability [26].

## Immutability

One of the key characteristics of Blockchain is the creation of immutable ledgers. Any centrally located database is vulnerable to fraud and hacking since it relies on a third-party intermediary for security. Like Bitcoin, blockchain keeps its ledgers up to date indefinitely. Each node in the system keeps a copy of the digital ledger. Every node must validate a transaction's legitimacy before adding it. It is entered into the ledger if the majority believes it to be valid. Blockchain is immutable because of cryptographic hashes, which is one of its essential components. Hash's primary benefit is that it cannot be reverse engineered. That explains why it is so well-liked. The Secure Hash Algorithm 256 (SHA-256) is the most often used hash function. Another reality is that once transaction blocks are put to the ledger, they cannot be changed by anyone afterwards. As a result, no user on the network will have access to edit or delete or update it.

## Network Speed

Traditional banking systems require extensive settlement time and can take days to complete, they move at an incredibly slow pace. This is among the primary justifications for why major banking institutions need to modernize their banking systems. The blockchain, which can settle money transfers at incredibly quick rates, can help us overcome this problem. However, this is not the sole benefit as the speed of a blockchain varies depending on whether it is a public, private, or consortium blockchain. The end result is that these institutions ultimately save a great deal of time and money, and the consumer also benefits from the convenience.

## Consensus Mechanism

The very efficient nature of Blockchain technologies is due to the consensus algorithm (Figure 5). It is a differentiating quality and a crucial part of every blockchain. Simply explained, consensus is the group of active nodes on the network's decision-making process. The nodes can reach an agreement in this situation relatively quickly.

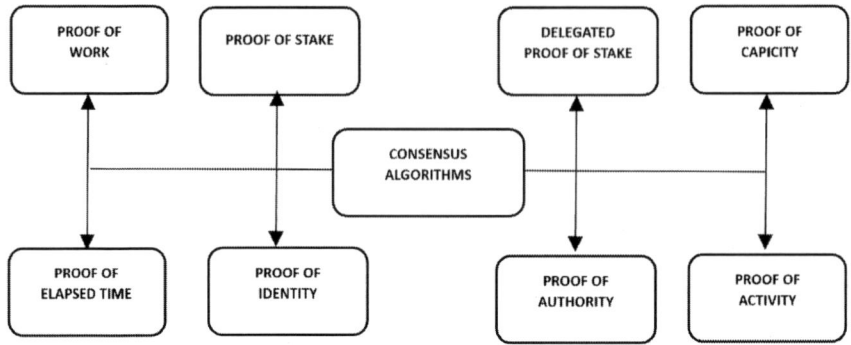

**Figure 5**. Types of Consensus Algorithms.

For a system to function properly when millions of nodes are validating a transaction, a consensus is unavoidably required. It may be compared to a voting process where the majority wins and the minority is required to support it. In fact, it is unanimity that makes the system unreliable. Furthermore, the blockchain-based distributed network ensures that every node has a copy of the data, and it would not be possible for the attacker to modify the content in each and every copy within the network. The algorithms that on which the blockchain can be trusted even if the nodes do not trust one another. Because of this, every action taken on the network favors the blockchain. Figure 5 depicts the various types of consensus algorithms.

### *Tamper Proof Data*

Data that is tamper-resistant can withstand any harm or interference, whether deliberate or unintentional, to the data, system, or any product. The blockchain is believed to be tamper-resistant, which means that the data being kept or generated on its blocks can never, under any circumstances, be altered or tampered with, neither during the generation process nor later [27]. The information may be tampered with in one of two situations: either when the miner attempts to change the data, or when the adversary makes such an attempt. A blockchain-based ecosystem allows for the control of tampering because the transactions are protected by digital signatures and the hash function. Additionally, the transaction is verified by the network nodes through mining. In this scenario, the first problem is dealt with since a miner trying to alter the content or fudge the signature would be unable to do so because he lacks the request generator's private key [27]. The hash pointer and cryptography would be used in the second scenario, where an adversary tries to tamper with the data. The hashes of the other blocks would be impacted if someone attempted to modify the contents, resulting in a mismatch in the hash values. In addition, the blockchain based distributed network ensures that each node has a copy of the data, making it impossible for an attacker to alter the data in each and every copy inside the network. Conclusively, it is impossible to tamper with the data within the blockchain network without being noticed [28].

## Use Case of Blockchain Technology

### *Health Care Industries*

A blockchain network is applied in the healthcare sector to store and share patient data across hospitals, diagnostic labs, pharmaceutical companies, and physicians/doctors. Blockchain applications can precisely detect serious errors, including potentially deadly ones, in the medical industry. In the healthcare sector, it can therefore enhance the efficiency, security, and transparency of sharing medical data. Medical institutions can acquire insight and improve the analysis of patient information with the use of this technology. In this essay, we looked at blockchain technology and its important advantages for the healthcare industry as depicted in Figure 6. Diagrams are used to discuss how blockchain technology may help global healthcare through its various capabilities, enablers, and unified work-flow process?

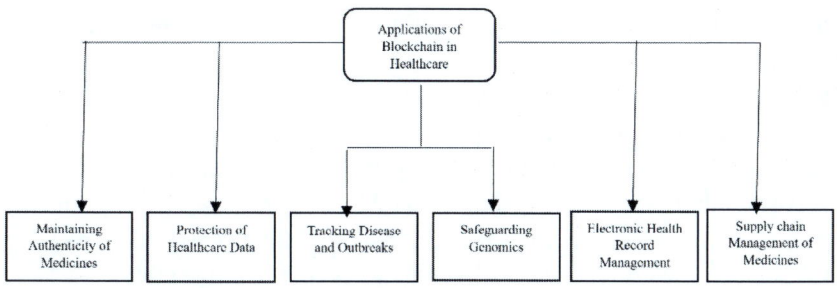

Figure 6. Various applications of Blockchain in Healthcare Sector.

Clinical trial fraud is also handled effectively by blockchain, and this technology's potential here is to increase data efficiency for the healthcare industry. It can provide a distinctive data storage pattern at the greatest level of security and lessen the concern about data tampering in healthcare. It offers adaptability, connectivity, accountability, and authentication for access to data. Health records must be kept secure and private for a number of reasons. Blockchain helps prevent specific dangers and provides decentralized data protection for the healthcare industry. Figure 6 depicts a few applications of Blockchain in the area of healthcare.

*Data Privacy*
There has recently been an upsurge in reported instances of security issues involving users' personal data. As a result, a third party has control over the data and will gather all personal data. Blockchain can do away with this middleman and enable direct transactions between two parties. In our world, data volume has recently increased. The largest online social network, Facebook, accumulated 300 petabytes of personal information. Sensitive or personal information shouldn't be safe in the hands of strangers. They are being abused and attacked. Blockchain enables users to operate independently of third parties. Blockchain acknowledges users as the proprietors of their private information. Blockchain needs its own set of guidelines and rules. It's referred to as a smart contract. The gateway keeper should establish some regulations and have them documented in a contract before initiating a transaction. Peer to peer communication will result. Bitcoin has shown that it is trustworthy, and that computing is possible in a decentralized network in the financial sector. Bitcoin is a type of digital currency, and blockchain is mostly suggested for handling it.

*Supply Chain Management*
Real-time tracking of commodities as they move and change hands across the supply chain is one of the activities that blockchain is particularly suited for due to its immutable record. The use of a blockchain expands the possibilities available to businesses that deliver these items. It is possible to schedule supply chain activities using entries on a blockchain, such as allocating recently delivered products to various shipping containers. Blockchain provides a novel and flexible method of organizing and utilizing tracking data to guarantee the security of the commodities.

## *Electronic Healthcare Records (EHRs)*

Blockchain deals with several frameworks for managing authenticity, secrecy, and accountability in the processing of electronic medical records. It primarily comes into play while processing sensitive data. Blockchain will operate as a decentralized program for online electronic records. Every application in a centralized system ought to be completed in one place. However, in a decentralized setting, application development should take place elsewhere.

Some difficulties and restrictions should be lessened by using electronic medical records. When implementing a privately managed system, this system will encounter some significant obstacles. So, instead of using provider or hospital records, you would use your own records. To honor the existing data, a portion of the privately controlled records would be downloaded into the institutional record. Blockchain enables the avoidance of these difficulties. Because a significant exchange-based transaction between two parties is led by blockchain. They don't reveal their identities to anyone else. One public key and one private key should be shared by each and every user (or patient) on a blockchain.

## *Decentralized Applications (DApps)*

A decentralized application, or DApp, is comparable to the digital apps accessible on smartphones and laptops, but it uses blockchain technology to keep user data out of the hands of third parties and the companies behind it. DApps are decentralized apps, same as bitcoin is decentralized money. The blockchain simultaneously keeps copies of its growing data stack on a large number of collaborating computers known as "nodes." These machines are owned by users, not the DApp's authors or creators [28].

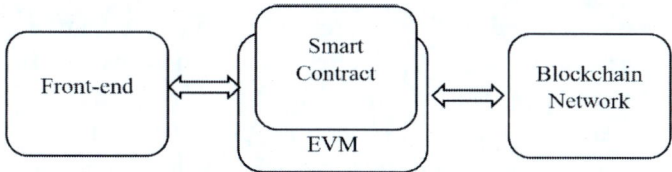

**Figure 7.** Architecture of a Decentralized Application.

DApps, like traditional apps, may provide social networks, gaming, entertainment, productivity tools, and so on. Many are intended to serve as tools to assist customers in gaining access to decentralized financial services, like DeFi (Decentralized Finance) [29]. In summary, a DApp, or decentralized application, is a software program that operates on a distributed network. It is hosted on a peer-to-peer decentralized network rather than a centralized server. Figure 7 depicts the architecture on which today's most popular DApps are made up of.

- *Smart Contracts*: A smart contract, often referred to as a cryptocurrency contract, is a piece of computer software that, under specific conditions, controls directly and automatically how digital assets are transferred between the parties. A smart contract functions similarly to a conventional contract, with automatic contract enforcement. Smart contracts are computer programs that run exactly as their authors have coded or programmed them too. Smart contracts are enforceable by code, just as traditional contracts are enforceable by law.
- *Ethereum*: To securely execute and validate smart contract application code, Ethereum is a decentralized blockchain platform (or DApps). Participants can conduct business using smart contracts without the need for a trustworthy central authority. Due to the immutability, verifiability, and safe distribution of transaction records over the network, participants fully own and have access to all transaction data. User-created Ethereum accounts can both send and receive transactions, as a cost of processing transactions on the network, a sender must sign transactions and use Ether i.e., Ethereum native coin [29]. Using the native Solidity scripting language and Ethereum Virtual Machine, Ethereum provides a remarkably flexible platform on which to develop decentralized apps. The robust ecosystem of developer tools and well-established best practices that have emerged with the protocol's maturation are beneficial to decentralized application developers that implement smart contracts on Ethereum. This maturity also extends to the standard of the user-experience for users of Ethereum apps, with wallets like Metalmark, Argent, Rainbow, and others providing simple user interfaces through which to interact with the Ethereum blockchain and the smart contracts implemented there. Ethereum's large user base motivates programmers to publish their creations on the network, further establishing Ethereum as the preferred platform for decentralized applications like DeFi and NFTs.

## Copyright and Licensing

In the creative industries, such as music, filmmaking, etc., copyright and royalties are major problems. These are artistic forms of expression, and it doesn't appear that they relate in any way to blockchain. Nevertheless, this technology is crucial for ensuring security and openness in the creative sectors as well. There are innumerable instances of plagiarism in music, films, and other artistic mediums in which the original creators are not given credit. Blockchain, which keeps a comprehensive ledger of artist rights, can be utilized to rectify this situation. Additionally transparent, blockchain can offer a safe record of artist royalties and agreements with major production corporations. Digital currencies like Bitcoin can also be used to administer royalty payments [30].

Apart from the daily use case mentioned above, blockchain technology is used in various other industries, including big data, cybersecurity, international payments, capital markets, trade finance, real estate, and power grids and cryptocurrencies and much more (Figure 8).

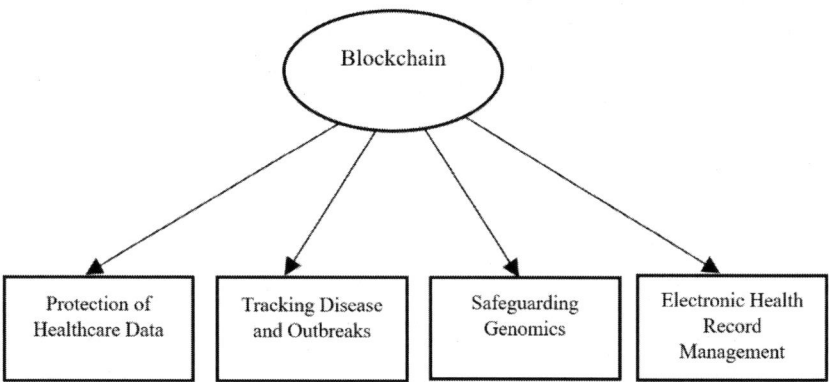

**Figure 8**. Applications of Blockchain Technology.

## Conclusion

Due to its characteristics that ensure secure, transparent, and private data transfers between peers in a distributed network, blockchain technology was initially presented as the foundation for the first digital currency and is currently being used in a wide range of application sectors. The blockchain is an incredibly safe framework for conducting data transactions without any middlemen because to its features like time-stamped data, digital signatures, consensus mechanisms, cryptographic hashing, etc. In addition, the blockchain provides features like pseudo identity, tamper-resistance, data consistency, and confidentiality, among others that guarantee the security and privacy of the data on the network, hence strengthening the security of the blockchain system. A detailed examination of the blockchain application, including its security characteristics is presented in this paper. For upcoming work, we can focus on one application or a particular blockchain and delve deeply into its architecture to analyze blockchain security from the standpoint of the blockchain architecture used in that application or chain.

## References

[1] *A Survey of blockchain security issue and challenges* (Iuon-Chang Lin and Tzu-Chun Liao) [jan-12- 2017].

[2] Ichikawa, D., Kashiyama, M., Ueno, T. Tamper-resistant mobile health using blockchain technology. *JMIR mHealth uHealth* 2017, 5, e111.

[3] Nugent, T., Upton, D., Cimpoesu, M. Improving data transparency in clinical trials using blockchain smart contracts. *F1000Research* 2016, 5, 2541.

[4] Muzammal, M., Qu, Q., Nasrulin, B. Renovating blockchain with distributed databases: An open source system. *Futur. Gener. Comput. Syst.* 2019, 90, 105–117.

[5] Azaria, A., A. Ekblaw, T. Vieira, and A. Lippman, Medrec: Using blockchain for medical data access andpermission management, in *2016 2nd International Conference on Open and Big Data* (OBD), Aug 2016, pp. 2530.

[6] https://www.researchgate.net/publication/319058582 *Blockchain Challenges and Opportunities A Survey.*

[7] http://www.meti.go.jp/english/press/2016/pdf/053101f.pdf.

[8] https://www.dotmagazine.online/issues/innovation-in-digital-commerce/what-can-blockchain-do/security-and-privacy-in-blockchain-environments.

[9] Li, X., Jiang, P., Chen, T., Luo, X., Wen, Q. A survey on the security of blockchain systems. *Futur. Gener. Comput. Syst.* 2020, 107, 841–853.

[10] Kavita Saini. "Next Generation Logistics: A Novel Approach of Blockchain Technology," *Essential Enterprise Blockchain Concepts and Applications*, CRC Press, USA, 2020, ISBN: 9781003097990.

[11] Narayanan, Neethu, K. P. Arjun, Kavita Saini "A Blockchain Technology for Asset Management in Multinational Operation," *Essential Enterprise Blockchain Technology and Applications*, to be published by CRC Press Taylor & Francis, 2020, ISBN: 9781003097990.

[12] Pethuru Raj Chelliah and Kavita Saini, "Expounding the Blockchain Architecture," *Blockchain and IoT Integration: Approaches and applications* to be published by CRC Press Taylor & Francis, 2021.
[13] Zyskind, G., Nathan O. and Pentland A. 2015 Decentralizing privacy: Using blockchain to protect personal data in Security and Privacy Workshops (SPW), *2015 IEEE* May.
[14] Boneh D., and M. K. Franklin, "Identity-based encryption from the Weil pairing," in *Advances in Cryptology-CRYPTO*, Springer Berlin Heidelberg, vol. 2139, 2001, pp. 213–229.
[15] Lewko, A., and B. Waters, "Unbounded HIBE and Attribute-Based Encryption," in *Advances in Cryptology - EUROCRYPT 2011*, Springer Berlin Heidelberg, vol. 6632, 2011, pp. 547–567.
[16] Fotiou, N., and G. C. Polyzos, "Decentralized name-based security for content distribution using blockchains," in *2016 IEEE Conference on Computer Communications Workshops* (INFOCOM WKSHPS), San Francisco, CA, 2016, pp. 415-420.
[17] Asghar, M. R., M. Ion, G. Russello, and B. Crispo, "Securing data provenance in the cloud," in *Open Problems in Network Security*, Springer, 2012, pp. 145–160.
[18] Liang, X., S. Shetty, D. Tosh, C. Kamhoua, K. Kwiat, and L. Njilla, "Prov Chain : A Blockchain-Based Data Provenance Architecture in Cloud Environment with Enhanced Privacy and Availability," in *17th IEEE/ACM International Symposium on Cluster, Cloud and Grid Computing (CCGRID)*, Madrid, Spain, 2017, pp. 468-477.
[19] Kavita, Saini, Shivansh Sharma, Utsav Sarkar, Aakash Chabaque, "Blockchain and Cryptography," *4th IEEE International Conference on Advances in Computing, Communication Control and Networking* (ICAC3N–22), Paper ID : 117, 16-17 Dec. 2022, ISBN : 978-1-6654-7436-8, Publication Year: 2022, Page(s) :1863-1868.
[20] http://www.blockchain4innovation.it/wp-content/uploads/sites/4/2017/05/ Blockchain-.
[21] https://www.coindesk.com/information/who-created-ethereum.
[22] https://www.statista.com/statistics/647523/worldwide-bitcoin-blockchain-size.
[23] *SegWit2x backers cancel plans for bitcoin hard fork*, 2017. Available online : https://techcrunch.com/2017/11/08/segwit2x-backers-cancel-plansfor-bitcoin-hard-fork/. (Accessed 1 February 2018).
[24] Sasson, E. B., A. Chiesa, C. Garman, M. Green, I. Miers, E. Tromer, M. Virza, Zerocash: decentralized anonymous payments from bitcoin, in : *Security and Privacy (SP), 2014 IEEE Symposium on*, San Jose, CA, USA, IEEE, 2014, pp. 459–474.
[25] Miers, I., C. Garman, M. Green, A. D. Rubin, Zerocoin: anonymous distributed e-cash from bitcoin, in : *Security and Privacy (SP), 2013 IEEE Symposium on*, Berkeley, CA, USA, IEEE, 2013, pp. 397–411.
[26] *Monero*, 2017. https://getmonero.org/. (Accessed 20 October 2017).
[27] *Bitcoin Fog*, 2017. Available online : http://bitcoinfog.info/. (Accessed 1 February 2018).

[28] Maxwell, G. CoinJoin: bitcoin privacy for the real world, in : *Post on Bitcoin Forum*, 2013 Available online : https://bitcointalk.org/index.php?topic=279249.msg2983902#msg2983902. (Accessed 1 February 2018).

[29] Greenberg, A. *'Dark Wallet' is about to make Bitcoin money laundering easier than ever*, 2014. URL http://www.wired.com/2014/04/dark-wallet.

[30] Telang, Samir, Arvind Chel, Anant Nemade, and Geetanjali Kaushik. "Intelligent transport system for a Smart City." In *Security and Privacy Applications for Smart City Development*, pp. 171-187. Springer, Cham, 2021.

## Chapter 2

# An Extensive Study of Blockchain Technology: Privacy Perspective

**Brijesh Kumar Bhardwaj[1],\*, PhD**
**Kavita Srivastava[2], PhD**
**Anshul Mishra[3], PhD**
**and J. N. Singh[4], PhD**

[1]Dept. of MCA, Dr. R. M. L. Avadh University, Ayodhya, Uttar Pradesh, India
[2]Department of Business Management and Entrepreneurship,
Dr. R. M. L. Avadh University, Ayodhya, Uttar Pradesh, India
[3]Department of Computer Applications, LBSGCM, Lucknow, Uttar Pradesh, India
[4]Galgotias University, Gr. Noida, Uttar Pradesh, India

## Abstract

Blockchain technology has seen wide appropriation and quick development as of late. Initially, this chapter explains the specialized qualities and then the specialized points of interest of blockchain. Secondly, the security model of the blend of blockchain and hash capacity, tokens, and Coinbase is quickly depicted, and the work process of blockchain is dissected. Privacy ensures that data can't be perused by unapproved clients. Privacy gives clients the property of controlling the openness of data.

A blockchain is a shared and appropriate record that energizes the path toward recording and following assets without the need for a single, consolidated course of action. It permits two get-togethers to pass on and trade assets in a shared organization where scattered decisions are made

---

\* Corresounding Author's Email: wwwbkb2012@gmail.com

In: Blockchain and EHR
Editors: Kavita Saini, Amar Kumar and J. N. Singh
ISBN: 979-8-89113-380-8
© 2024 Nova Science Publishers, Inc.

by the prevailing party as opposed to by a single concentrated position. It is probably secure against assaults planned to control the structure by bartering the focal regulator. Blockchain innovations are presently basically industry-driven, lending the field a somewhat unexpected angle in comparison to other regions of exploration.

Many organizations are now overseen by concentrated regulators, for example, a support authority. Hence, the organizations are slanted toward assaults on the bound-together regulator. Then again, blockchain is a well-thought-out and appropriate record that can help settle many of the issues with centralization.

**Keywords:** blockchain technology, blockchain challenges, data privacy

## Introduction

Blockchain is a new technology of developing significance as its ubiquity keeps on rising. Notwithstanding, misconceptions and misinterpretations of this new technology have ceaselessly exposed all members engaged with the technology to digital dangers as of late. Henceforth, this part investigated and broke down blockchain framework security episodes to comprehend blockchain framework with hash, blockchain, and conveyed framework, as well as to give a security assessment structure to blockchain frameworks.

With Bitcoin and its likes that are created by professionals rather than cryptographers, trust will in general be put not in conventional proofs and properties but rather in functional resistance to assaults dependent on normal information and experience by specialists [2]. What follows from this plan is a constant smoothness of proposed arrangements, just as in the absence of normal, brought-together plan decisions and measures. Accordingly, there are plenty of arrangements that each guarantee to be the best arrangement. It will be fascinating to see how the field advances and what winds up being picked as the brilliant standard; however, any guarantee of stability is in the distant future, particularly in more trial blockchains, for example, side chains. In blockchain stockpiling technology, the capacity of the square resembles an accounting layer, which can record all the data trades in the general blockchain, and these data records can be checked by different hubs constantly. Unique to the overall method of record, the data record of blockchain is dissipated in all hubs without focus, which comprises a regular appropriated database framework. At the point when a few hubs are assaulted

# An Extensive Study of Blockchain Technology: Privacy Perspective

or data is harmed, different hubs won't affect the framework since they have flawless data [3].

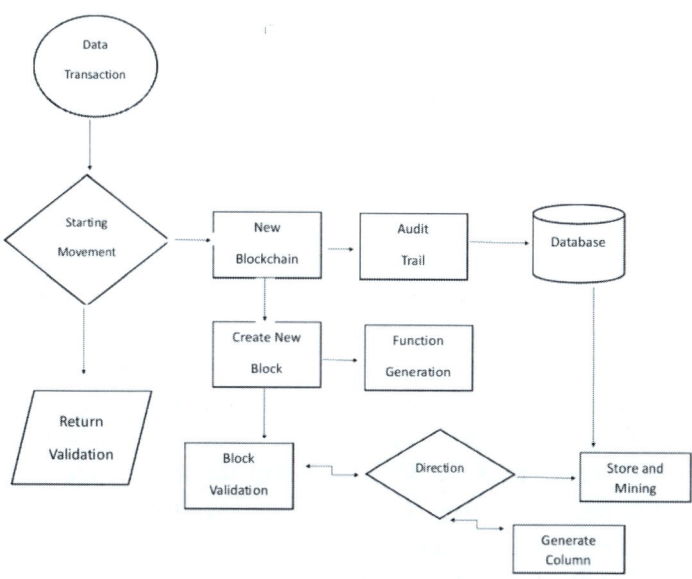

**Figure 1.** Blockchain Work Steps.

## How Does Blockchain Work?

For an investigation of the technology, this segment portrays how blockchain works from a significant point of view. The principal cycle in blockchain is adding exchange records to a public record that runs down past exchanges [4]. The total number of records is alluded to as a square. The public record of past exchanges is known as the blockchain, as it is a chain of squares. The blockchain is responsible for checking with the organization that an exchange has happened. A hub (client) on the blockchain network confirms the legitimacy of the exchange and forestalls endeavors to abuse or adjust authentic data exchanges. As appeared in Figure 1, the cycle inside the blockchain is separated into different stages, beginning with the solicitation of data exchange and giving the total guidance in Figure 1: blockchain work steps.

## Applications of Blockchain Technology

The following section presents some of the practical applications of blockchain technology in various areas. Applications have been sorted into the accompanying gatherings: smart contracts, government, financial industry, accounting, and business process management.

- Smart Contract: A smart contract is planned to promise one assembling that the counterparty will fulfill his certifications with confirmation [5]. The blockchain intends to dispense with sellers for exchanges. Generally, this outsider is responsible for keeping up and executing the agreements and assembling the trust between any elaborate gatherings. In this way, brilliant contracts can vanquish moral danger issues, for instance, fundamental default, and they can altogether decrease the costs of affirmation and approval.
- Contract Management: Blockchain technology in contract management offers a response for associations affirming arrangement data that could be incredibly profitable for affiliations and attempts by a wide scope of associations, for instance, in specialized ventures and development [6].
- Blockchain Internet-of-Things (IoT) is a plan of interconnected, mechanical, and progressed machines, things, animals, or people that are outfitted with fascinating identifiers with the ability to move data over an association without anticipating that humans should human or human-to-PC correspondence.

## Hash Function

The hash function is an important part of many cryptographic algorithms. A significant part of blockchain technology is applying hash work to some tasks. Hashing is a strategy for applying hash capacity to data that registers a generally one-of-a-kind yield for practically any size of information. It permits people to freely get input data and hash data and produce similar outcomes, demonstrating that the data remained unaltered. A hash work is just a capacity that takes in information esteem, and from that information, a yield esteem deterministic of the information esteem for any x information value, the yield will consistently get a similar y yield value at whatever point the hash work is run. Thus, every piece of information has a decided yield. As appeared in Figure 2, a hash work is subsequently something that takes information (which can be any data, for example, numbers, documents, and so on) and yields a hash. A hash is normally shown as a hexadecimal number. These are diverse hash calculations; for example, MD and SHA are the most famous hash capacities [7]. Hash limits are all around irreversible (single course), which infers that one can't figure out the data if they simply know the yield—aside from endeavoring for each possible piece of data [8]. There are numerous applications for hash works, yet data decency or trustworthiness checking is the most essential application [9].

## Experimental Analysis

In the current computational environment, data is captured from different sources and sent among gadgets through organizations. Its subsidiaries have been utilized as useful assets to investigate and deal with the caught data to accomplish viable thinking intending to the concerns regarding security. Peer A analyzes the steps in three or more segments with two levels.

## Network-Based Observation

A key element of blockchain technology lives in its disseminated nature [10]. Unique about concentrated and decentralized organizations, Figure 3 shows the distinction between these three organizational structures. A disseminated processing network framework is where data and assets are spread out on different equipment hubs. It is organized as a shared organization on top of the Internet. The term friend, or P2P, infers that the PCs that participate in the association are allied to each other, that they are by and large the same, and that there are no exceptional centers [11]. All association center points share the effort of providing association organizations, where centers give and use the organizations at a similar time. Conveyance of control in blockchain technology and Bitcoin applications is a central rule that must be accomplished and kept up by P2P network engineering. In addition, in a blockchain situation, every hub keeps a database (ledger) of every single substantial exchange, which is sent among the hubs in the organization. Regardless of whether each hub holds a duplicate of the record, only those clients that hold the mark on it can get to the data [12]. In any case, these compartments are fixed, and their substance must be seen by the individuals who hold the consent [13]. The blockchain is characterized as a chain of squares with data associated with it, utilizing cryptographic hashes. A square may contain exchanges between numerous clients and, for the most part, is openly available to all customers of the association. Likewise, each square (block) contains the hash of the past square and the trade data, thus making a secured and unchanging, simply connected chain.

The essential thought behind the utilization of square chain frameworks is to provide a flaw-open-minded circulated processing framework where authority could be dispersed without having trust in the focal framework, which depends on hash conversion (Figure 4). It enables the building of previous key and hash key infrastructures for an enormous number of untrusted members. The issue with the square chain framework is that it is inclined to single-point failure, and the framework doesn't give straightforwardness, reasonable admittance to assets, trustworthiness, non-renouncement of exchanges performed, or data permanence [14].

## Coinbase Transaction

The blockchain, which is a conveyed record of exchanges (Figure 5), grew initially as the bookkeeping stage for the virtual currency Bitcoin. The technology is utilized to check exchanges, making records that can't be changed or erased with hashes and past keys. Check is refined in a decentralized way through an organization of members, or dispersed hubs, instead of through vendor company involvement, for example, in the transactions of any bank. An exploration of blockchain cannot begin without understanding Bitcoin, because it is the first application built on blockchain. It is somewhat odd that Bitcoin became mainstream before the underlying technology did.

**Figure 2.** Hash Involvement.

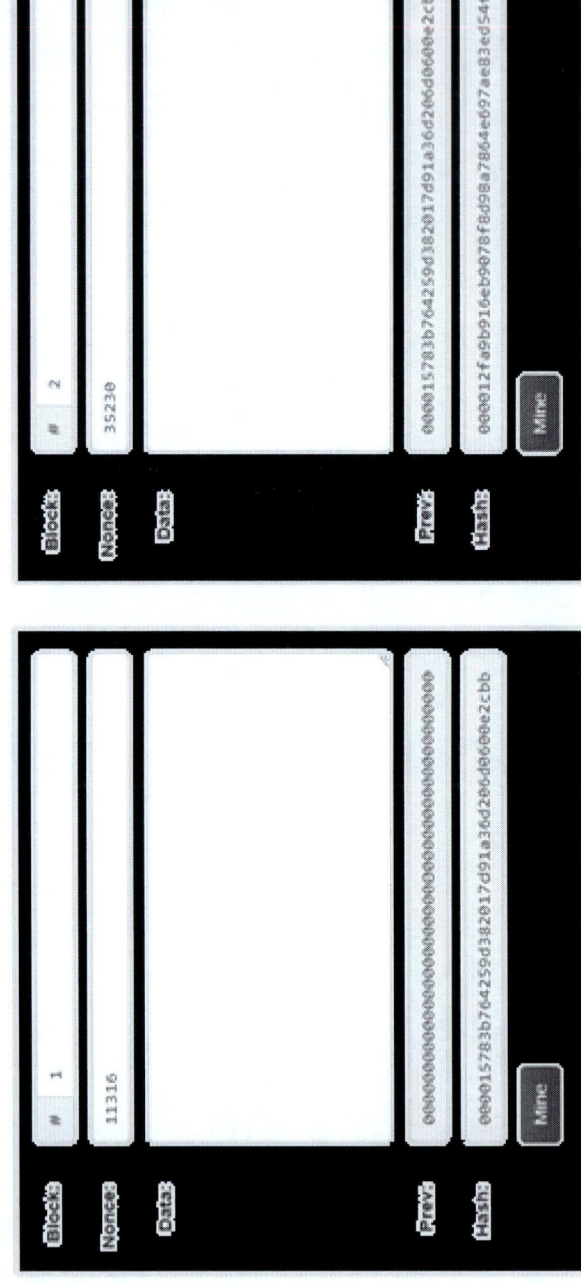

**Figure 3.** Blockchain Evaluation Step_1 With Hash Function.

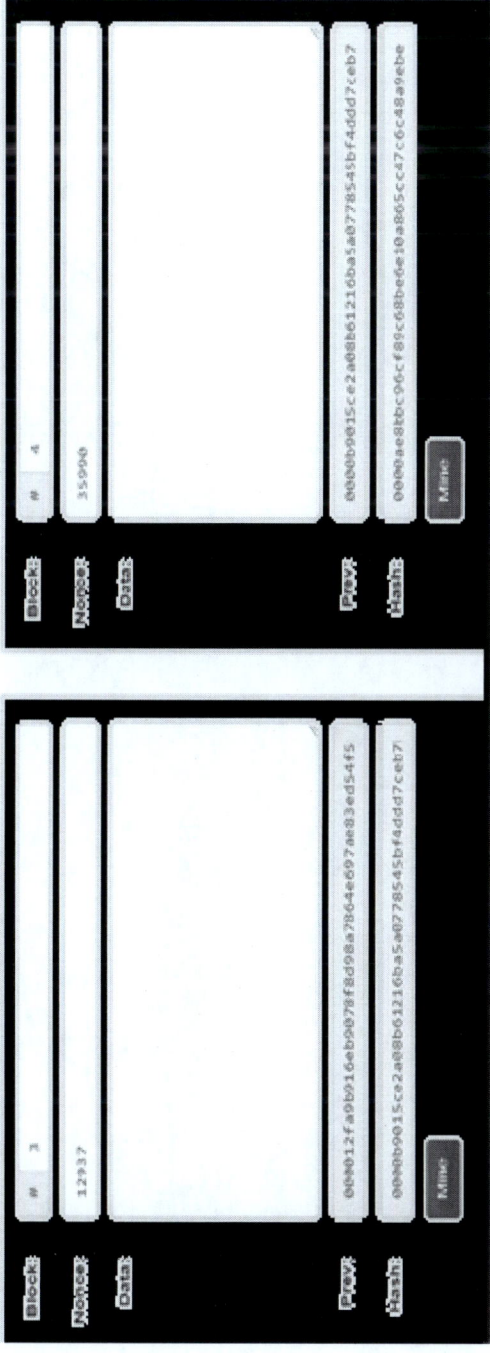

**Figure 4.** Blockchain Evaluation Step_2 With Hash Function.

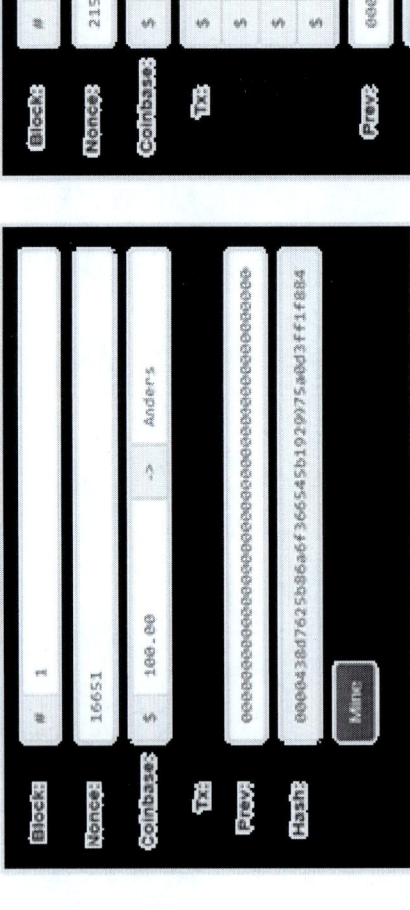
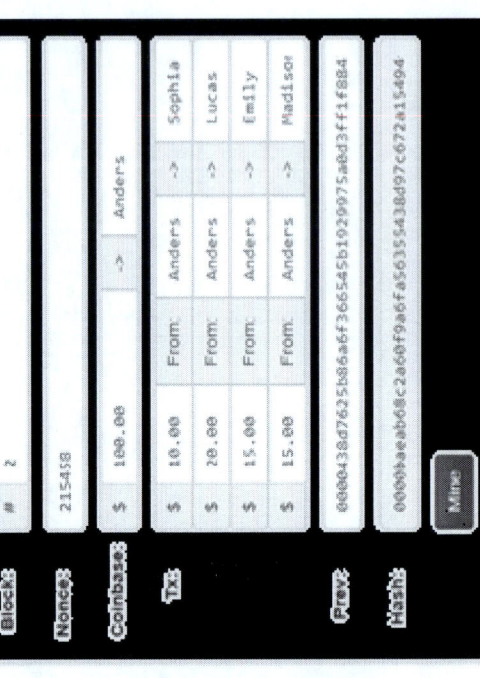

**Figure 5.** Coinbase Transaction Structure.

## Conclusion

Considering the past section, we have picked up a decent comprehension of what the blockchain is and why it is required. Hence, it is time to expand on top of that to see how the blockchain functions. This part will be founded on the specialized definition given by the analyst, who characterized blockchain as a stage with a critical outcome. Consequently, the connected specialized ideas will be examined as independent perceptions; at that point, we will wrap them all up utilizing a model as represented in this part of the section.

*Observation 1*: Blockchain technology conveyed numerous focal points over existing innovations. Be that as it may, the two primary qualities offered are trust and decentralization.

*Observation 2*: A smart contract can execute and implement the presentation of an exchange agreement.

*Observation 3*: There is a blockchain in the production network, and it would apply to exchanges.

*Observation 4*: The specialized test is that blockchain technology can't ensure data dependability in the account and needs work in this direction.

*Observation 5*: Blockchain innovation may present this necessary trust with straightforward exchanges, notwithstanding a record of the item, so the client knows the genuine estimation of the item.

## References

[1] Ahram T., A. Sargolzaei, S. Sargolzaei, J. Daniels, B. *Amaba Blockchain technology innovations 2017 IEEE Technology and Engineering Management Society Conference*, TEMSCON 2017 (2017), pp. 137-141.
[2] Chapron, G. (2017). The environment needs crypto governance. *Nature*, 545 (7655).
[3] Cocco, L., Pinna, A., & Marchesi, M. (2017). Banking on blockchain : Costs savings thanks to the blockchain technology. *Future Internet*, 9 (3), 25.
[4] Huckle, S., & White, M. (2016). Socialism and the blockchain. *Future Internet*, 8 (4), 49.
[5] Ishmaev, G. (2017). Blockchain technology as an institution of property. *Metaphilosophy*, 48 (5), 666-686.
[6] Lu, Q., & Xu, X. (2017). *Adaptable blockchain-based systems: A case study for product traceability*. IEEE Software, 34 (6), 21-27.
[7] Maxwell, D., Speed, C., & Pschetz, L. (2017). Story blocks : Reimagining narrative through the blockchain. *Convergence : The International Journal of Research into New Media Technologies*, 23 (1), 79 97.

[8] Xu X., I. Weber, M. Staples, *"Architecture for Blockchain Applications,"* Springer International Publishing, 2019.
[9] Henly C., S. Hartnett, B. Endemann, B. Tejblum, D. S. Cohen, "Energizing the Future with Blockchain," *Energy Law Journal*, 39, 197–232, 2018.
[10] Leonard C., "Blocking the Blockchain," *International Financial Law Review*, April 2016, 35, 58–59, 2016.
[11] Xu X., I. Weber, M. Staples, L. Zhu, J. Bosch, L. Bass, C. Pautasso and P. Rimba, *A taxonomy of blockchain-based systems for architecture design, in Software Architecture (ICSA)*, 2017 IEEE International Conference on, IEEE, 2017, 243–252.
[12] Zhang L., Z. Cai and X. Wang, *Fakemask: a novel privacy preserving approach for smartphones*, IEEE Transactions on Network and Service Management, 13 (2016), 335–348.
[13] Saini, K. (Ed.). (2021). *Blockchain and IoT Integration: Approaches and applications*. CRC Press.
[14] Zheng X., Z. Cai, J. Li and H. Gao, *Location-privacy-aware review publication mechanism for local business service systems*, in INFOCOM 2017-IEEE Conference on Computer Communications, IEEE, IEEE, 2017, 1–9.

Chapter 3

# Proposed Evaluation Framework for Blockchain Technology

**Brijesh Kumar Bhardwaj[1],***
**Kavita Srivastava[2]**
**Neeraj Kumar Tiwari[3]**
**and J. N. Singh[4]**

[1]Dept. of MCA, Dr R M L Avadh University, Ayodhya
[2]Department of Business Management and Entrepreneurship,
Dr R M L Avadh University, Ayodhya
[3]BBAU Satellite Campus (a central university), Tikarmafi, Amethi
[4]Galgotias University Gr Noida

## Abstract

This work gives a cryptic situation of blockchain-based applications across various regions. The reason for this is to investigate the status of blockchain advancement and its crypto applications. A blockchain is a record of all occasions that have been executed and divided between partaking parties. Every exchange in people is checked by the agreement of a large share of the members in the framework. The standards of encryption innovation are presented quickly, for example, hash function, and cryptosystem that is the non-symmetric, computerized signature. The use of cryptography in all degrees of blockchain is dissected, including the information layer, network layer, and so on. Finally, another investigation of a blockchain-based cryptography stage is introduced tending to the flow hash plans, trailed by suggestions for future

---

* Corresponding Author's Email: wwwbkb2012@gmail.com.

In: Blockchain and EHR
Editors: Kavita Saini, Amar Kumar and J. N. Singh
ISBN: 979-8-89113-380-8
© 2024 Nova Science Publishers, Inc.

blockchain analysts and engineers. The presented chapter discusses the evaluation of blockchain technology.

**Keywords:** blockchain-based applications, cryptosystem, hash function

## Introduction

Blockchain technology advances secure figuring without experts in an open architecture. A blockchain is a distributed database that logs trade records in a progressive sequence of blocks. Peer networks and cryptography secure the blockchain. Blockchain technology is utilized in bit currency transactions, information sharing, record keeping, and other applications. Blockchain link blocks using hash codes from a hash function. Hash codes are hard to compromise in big networks, but hackers can always hack smaller networks. This technology provides the most secure file transport applications. M. R. Asghar et al. suggested a secured and decentralized file transfer application utilizing blockchain. This application describes the file-sharing application by making use of a private blockchain network, which is suitable for usage in more compact businesses [1]. K. K. Muniswamy and colleagues [2] [3] evaluated the execution of a variety of symmetric and ant-symmetric calculations by considering a variety of characteristics. These characteristics included encryption/decoding time as well as record size.

A couple of years before, a breakthrough emerged in the field of data innovation that appears to be an answer to all concerns and the beginning of another spectacular time. This innovation may be characterized as a game-changer. Since 2016, this breakthrough has been known as the blockchain, even though the major variation of this technology was initially created in [4], and the fundamental idea took its current shape by X. Liang successfully in position [5]. It should come as no surprise that blockchain is comprised of blocks; these blocks are added in sequential order, just like in the well-known game "Snake." From the perspective of utilitarianism, it can be described as a decentralized information base that does not have a focal position and that carries out accurate and irreversible information movement within a decentralized P2P network [6]. Figure 1 depicts various blockchain applications.

## Health

In the present life quiet doesn't prefer to uncover their treatment subtleties to pariah. In this situation, patients can utilize this innovation to keep all data from others. The blockchain can be used as a site, or convenient application [7]. Every party in a blockchain has two keys specifically private and public keys. This can be used for user-specific transactional purposes.

Patients can deal with electronic clinical records by utilizing blockchain innovation. A greater part of the medical care establishment ought not to permit the patient to get their clinical information. Patients are getting confused about the security of their clinical records [8]. This issue can be effectively tended to by blockchain. In taking care of electronic clinical records, blockchain should manage diverse edge work for dealing with verification, secrecy, and responsibility. Online electronic records in blockchain will function as a decentralized application. In an incorporated climate, all applications should be done in one region. However, decentralized application is there in various areas.

## Financial

Current e-payment structures rely upon trusted, central pariahs to manage portions securely. The strain of diminishing the cost incurred on each transaction has prompted the banks to begin to acknowledge claims from one another. This innovation has facilitated traders as now they can manage and transact online from one account to another, thus removing the process of depositing hard cash to accounts [9]. Where note affirmation was confined to not many banks, this could be dealt with individually. As the number of banks in the structure extended, bank exchanges ended up being clumsier, and the rousing power for banks to make a more profitable system extended.

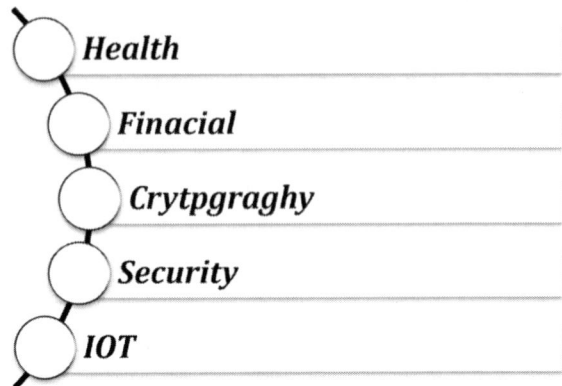

**Figure 1.** Blockchain Applications.

## Security

The blockchain innovation itself is still in the early stages of its rapid development, and its security is a significant distance behind the requirements of advancement at the present time. Both the exterior substances and the internal members could potentially be the source of the danger. The unmistakable quality of blockchain establishes new requirements for the security and security confirmation of data accumulation, transmission, and applications, and it also introduces new challenges to preexisting security arrangements, validation components, information insurance, protection assurance, and the regulation of information. In this day and age of widespread cybercrime, the significance of security concerns regarding the innovation of blockchain technology cannot be overstated [10]. The concept of vendor company has been removed in this technology i.e., any business or transaction will be done directly between the two parties. This brings quicker, solid and secure methods for exchanges. Self-execution is another pillar of blockchain where the owner will make an understanding out of their items and once it meets a specific of buyers, it will be executed paying little heed to client input.

## IoT

They are IC-based sensors basically that gather clients close to home, sensitive data and send it over the web. This data is put away in the information bases of concentrated organizations. As this information uncovers the individual conduct of clients, the protection of clients is in danger as organizations dealing with this information can utilize it. The *Crystal Surveillance* program is a delineation of such protection abuse. Firmware is fundamentally a product program that dwells on IoT gadgets that handle the tasks performed by the gadget. Obsolete firmware can restrict the functionality of the gadget and can clear the route for digital assaults coming about programmers to gain admittance to devices easily [11].

## Blockchain Technology

This innovation offers incredible potential to cultivate different areas with its special blend of qualities, for instance, decentralization, unchanging nature, and straightforwardness. We see promising possible results in the use of this advancement for science and the academic network. This chapter shows why blockchain technology suits exceptionally open science. Up to this point, the most prominent thought the development got was through data from industry about the improvement of cryptographic forms of money. Models are Bitcoin, Litecoin, Dash, and Monaro, which all have exceptional market capitalizations1. Blockchain technology is not restricted to cryptocurrencies only. The said technology is arising in numerous different areas including healthcare, voting systems, designing, and many more [12].

It is difficult to audit the market of existing and orchestrated exercises since there is no thorough public database or chronicle for it. Further, the extent of dreams, thoughts, and models is persistently extending, which suggests that this survey can just give a preview and doesn't profess to be finished or comprehensive. Notwithstanding logical papers and a couple of books, huge consideration was given to articles and white papers made by blockchain lovers and designs and disseminated in different IT-related web resources. Blockchain itself is an extremely late zone of examination and there is no broad exploration directed so far in the region. Most conversations and new revelation distributions are occurring in various web gatherings or web journals, e.g., a unique paper on Bitcoin distributed at his site page was never investigated as a real coherent paper and didn't have the term "blockchain" in it. Today it is seen as one of the fundamental papers. There are different contemporary books about the blockchain, anyway most of them endeavor to abuse the commonness of cryptographic forms of moncy and are simply an accumulation of various Bitcoin depictions.

Various relevant literature has been studied and referred to during this research. It seems that this topic has novelty, and there are only a couple of distributions about how BT can be utilized to cultivate open science or science when all is said in done. In a writing audit about the utilization of BT in various spaces, the application field of science didn't get referenced as an application area.

## Blockchain

There are various blockchain definitions by various scholars, and as called attention to in [12], there is no single, all around the world agreed definition; therefore, it is basic to appreciate the central bits of blockchain. Some have the appraisal that blockchain innovation has not been characterized at this point [13]; thus, they use Bitcoin as a sort of viewpoint point and use its three principal parts – exchanges, agreement, and organization. Researchers [13] offer a definition, where the dispersed record is portrayed as a scattered database that can have different customers (centers), and blockchains. Researchers [13] are of practically identical evaluation, portraying blockchain as "a feature of the execution layer of a disseminated programming framework", whose design is to guarantee information integrity. According to [14], the main contrast between blockchain and standard data set is that blockchain is the improved information base with a type of robotized answer for new record adding, approving, and disseminating the data over the P2P network. A few scholars disregard more point-by-point portions of blockchain and spotlight simply on information honesty, for instance, [15] states that blockchain is just a cryptographically unquestionable rundown of information.

## Proposed Evaluation Steps

Blockchain is a forward-thinking innovation that will probably alter the outcome of computing and shake up some businesses by forcing them to come up with more creative solutions. It is public, there is no end to it, and the material it consists of can therefore be found in a variety of settings. Innovation gained enormous popularity because of the proliferation of digital forms of money; however, it has applications in a wide variety of domains apart from accounting. There is a flawed method for deciphering blockchain that reduces it to a series of cryptographically secured squares. A square is a representation of an information structure that contains three distinct parts: the information itself, the hash of the previous square, and the hash of both the data and the previous hash. As a result, there is a requirement for dependencies between blocks, which can be applied to the purpose of ensuring the integrity of the blockchain as a whole. If the information in any of the squares is modified, the corresponding hash will also be updated. Because of this, a winding effect will be triggered, and the hashes of the succeeding squares will become invalid. This is the reason why there is a consistent flow of trade on the blockchain. This system has the potential to be extremely helpful in contributing to online security arrangements in dangerous areas such as Internet of Things (IoT) devices, organizations, and information storage and transmission.

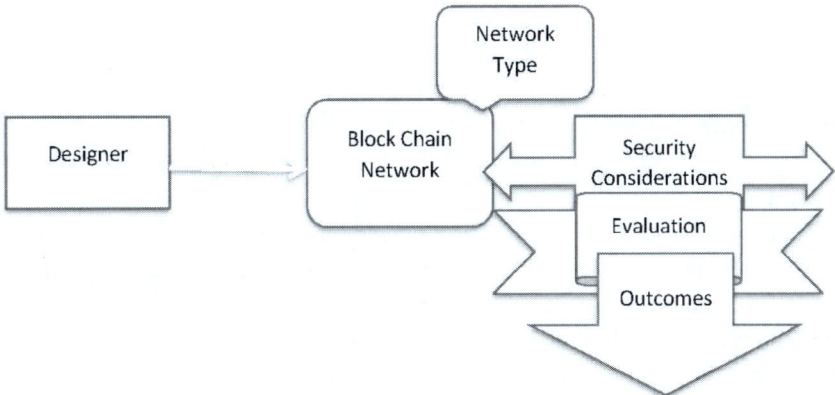

**Figure 2.** Security Architecture with Blockchain Technology.

The security architecture with the blockchain technology of the proposed structure appears in Figure 2. The registering hubs of the Sapiens Chain are decentralized and subsequently every hub won't be influenced by others. The clients present their assignments including site errands, application undertakings, and keen agreement assignments through the program, the mist hubs in Sapiens Chain initially recognize the sort of the assignment, and afterward, section undertakings into a few sections, running the calculations to choose appropriate hubs to manage the errand, lastly, assemble the outcomes into a documented form [15]. The system is appropriately centered around center functions: Identity, Protect, Detect, Respond, and Recover. Zeroing in on these center functions will help industry members create network safety programs for permissioned blockchains, giving specific accentuation to "anticipation" and the fuse of avoidance techniques inside the Protect, Detect, and Respond functions.

## Designers

In this stage, blockchain and digital currency are an extensive space to participate in. The result is a middle social occasion who are eagerly included and taken care of. In any case, to the typical individual or fashioner, outside of the exposure bubble, it's really hard to get empowered. There are so many new and hypothetical thoughts. There isn't any simple method to get included. The business has a terrible standing just like a scheme of quickly making the money. Designers have designed to complete the design with a set of rules and instructions below diagram as shown in Figure 3.

## Blockchain Network

The blockchain network is maintained by a peer-to-peer network. The organization comprises many PCs connected, and the task is broken into sub-tasks and shared among those PCs for execution. There is not, at this point one focal server, presently there are a few circulated and decentralized ones. Blockchain is considered by numerous individuals to be a disruptive core innovation. Although numerous scientists have understood the significance of blockchain, the exploration of blockchain is as yet at its outset. Subsequently, this work discusses various scholastic explorations on blockchain, particularly in the branch of knowledge of business and financial matters. Depending on the blockchain network from the service, we explore the complete issues about the network.

## Security Considerations

Another kind of security highlight is the chain of squares. In blockchain, each square ought to contain a hash esteem. These squares are related by their past hash. Expect an aggressor to come to address the data, by then its hash will be changed. It will impact the overall chain. Thus, it will grow the confirmation of fragile data or information. Blockchain innovation is a decentralized application. Chiefly it will uphold shared correspondence. Thus, an organization center is considered a PC. These gigantic numbers of centers should have a copy of the scattered record. This ought to check the trade. Odds are that if any of the centers differs a trade, by then it can't be continued [16].

**Evaluation**

For the most part, benchmarking on a blockchain has to take place in a climate that has been standardized, and it also needs an overall recorded outstanding burden as information. However, for public blockchain frameworks, it is tough to have fair control over the authentic extra weight and arrangement persons, which makes benchmarking an even greater challenge. This makes the benchmarking process more complex overall. Regarding the analysis of public blockchain, there are two possible configurations to consider. The primary plan is to create a private version of the associated testing organization and then use that to exert some influence over the existing benchmarks that were mentioned earlier to evaluate blockchain under the misleadingly planned remaining burdens. This requires an updated connector to be developed for either one of the two remaining tasks at hand or the blockchain network. An underlying mathematical analysis of the adaptability of Ethereum was led by Bez and colleagues. The findings indicate that Ethereum adheres to the flexibility trilemma, which asserts that it is extremely difficult for a blockchain platform to simultaneously demonstrate decentralization, adaptability, and security.

**Restored Outcomes**

As blockchain has developed to get increasingly more consideration, its presentation issues have gotten basic. To determine these issues, there have been numerous upgrades proposed, from framework-level advancement to new proficient agreement conventions and new accomplishments. Notwithstanding, such blockchain changes should be assessed in an important way to show their presentation favorable circumstances [16]. In this part, we present a methodology for covering existing blockchain execution assessment approaches and their assessment. From a significant level point of view, they can be arranged into experimental and scientific assessment methods.

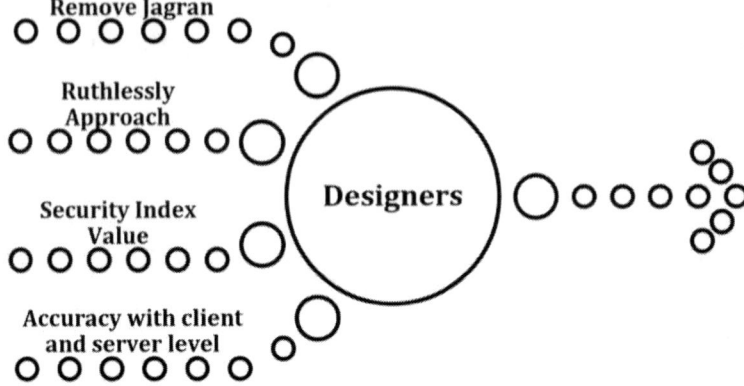

Figure 3. Essential Factors for Designers.

## Conclusion

In this chapter, the study on blockchain issues related to a security environment has been presented. These issues are chiefly security and protection related because of the absence of computational and capacity assets in security. In addition, blockchain can dispose of trust issues as needed in unified frameworks. This aids in saving protection and arrangement of non-merchant subordinate Firmware refreshes. Moreover, the integrity of data, the identity of devices, the fixed history of records, and access to the board to devices can be helpfully supervised through the association of blockchain. Notwithstanding the advantages, we likewise talked about some unintended execution issues like assessment steps of blockchain in security which give future bearings to scientists who are keen on this region. In light of the information, blockchain is a charming decision to manage typical issues being looked at by the environment. Keeping the feasible joint efforts in view, the mix of the two developments is needed to acquire insurgency in different fields of life.

## References

[1] Azaria, A., Ekblaw, A., Vieira, T., and Lippman, A. (2016). *Medrec: Using blockchain for medical data access and permission management in 2016 2nd International Conference on Open and Big Data (OBD)* 2530 Aug.

[2] Zyskind, G., Nathan, O. and Pentland, A. (2015). *Decentralizing privacy: Using blockchain to protect personal data in Security and Privacy Workshops (SPW)*, 2015 IEEE May.
[3] Boneh, D., and Franklin, M. K. (2001). "Identity-based encryption from the Weil pairing," in Advances in Cryptology-CRYPTO, Springer Berlin Heidelberg, vol. 2139, pp. 213–229.
[4] Lewko, A., and Waters, B. (2011). "Unbounded HIBE and Attribute-Based Encryption," in *Advances in Cryptology - EUROCRYPT 2011*, Springer Berlin Heidelberg, vol. 6632, pp. 547–567.
[5] Fotiou, N., and Polyzos, G. C. (2016). "Decentralized name-based security for content distribution using blockchains," in *2016 IEEE Conference on Computer Communications Workshops (INFOCOM WKSHPS)*, San Francisco, CA, pp. 415-420.
[6] Asghar, M. R., Ion, M., Russello, G., and Crispo, B. (2012). "Securing data provenance in the cloud," in Open Problems in Network Security, Springer, pp. 145–160.
[7] Pethuru Raj Chelliah and Kavita Saini, (2021). "Expounding the Blockchain Architecture", Blockchain and IoT Integration: Approaches and applications" to be published by CRC Press Taylor & Francis.
[8] Liang, X., Shetty, S., Tosh, D., Kamhoua, C., Kwiat, K., and Njilla, L. (2017). "Prov Chain: A Blockchain-Based Data Provenance Architecture in Cloud Environment with Enhanced Privacy and Availability," in *17th IEEE/ACM International Symposium on Cluster, Cloud and Grid Computing (CCGRID)*, Madrid, Spain, pp. 468-477.
[9] Kavita Saini, Shivansh Sharma, Utsav Sarkar, and Aakash Chabaque, (2022). "Blockchain and Cryptography", *4th IEEE International Conference on Advances in Computing, Communication Control and Networking (ICAC3N–22)*, 16-17 Dec. 2022, ISBN: 978-1-6654-7436-8, Publication Year: 2022, Page(s):1863 – 1868
[10] Saini, K. (2020). "Next Generation Logistics: A Novel Approach of Blockchain Technology", *Essential Enterprise Blockchain Concepts and Applications*, CRC Press, USA, ISBN: 9781003097990
[11] Muniswamy-Reddy, K. K., Holland, D. A., Braun, U., and Seltzer, M. I. (2006). "Provenance-aware storage systems." in USENIX Annual Technical Conference, General Track, pp. 43–56.
[12] Asghar, M. R., Ion, M., Russello, G., and Crispo, B. (2012). "Securing data provenance in the cloud," in Open Problems in Network Security, Springer, pp. 145–160.
[13] Miers, I., Garman, C., Green, M., Rubin, A. D. (2013). Zerocoin: anonymous distributed e-cash from bitcoin, in: Security and Privacy (SP), 2013 IEEE Symposium on, Berkeley, CA, USA, IEEE, pp. 397–411.
[14] Saini, K. (Ed.). (2021). *Blockchain and IoT Integration: Approaches and applications*. CRC Press.
[15] Dutta, S., and Saini, K. (2022). Blockchain Implementation Using Python. In *Advancing Smarter and More Secure Industrial Applications Using AI, IoT, and Blockchain Technology* (pp. 123-136). IGI Global.

[16] Kumari, K., and Saini, K. (2019). Cfdd (counterfeit drug detection) using blockchain in the pharmaceutical industry. *Int J Eng Res Technol (IJERT)*, 8, 1-4.

Chapter 4

# Online Voting System on a Secure Platform - Blockchain

**Bankuri Singhal**[*]
**Mahesh Kuma**[†]
**Poras Khaterpal**[‡]
**Prakhar Priyadarshi**[§]
**and Mohit Dayal**[‖]
Department of Information Technology, Bharati Vidyapeeth College of Engineering, Paschim Vihar, New Delhi, India

## Abstract

Every country must have a simple voting process that satisfies the needs of the public in order to give the right person power. Additionally, there are several serious problems with the present traditional voting procedures, such as a lack of security and transparency. A distributed ledger can be used to build an easy-to-use and reliable system for handling and storing any digital data. Therefore, blockchain technology was established on the foundation of a distributed ledger. This chain is secured using cryptographic and hashing techniques, making it incredibly challenging for an unauthorized user to access the data. It became apparent that blockchain technology can be applied to many different types of activities, such as electronic voting. Many universities

---

[*] Corresponding Auhtor's Email: rohtak.bankuri01@gmail.com.
[†] Corresponding Author's Email: malkanimahesh@gmail.com.
[‡] Corresponding Author's Email: porask@gmail.com.
[§] Corresponding Author's Email: priyadarshi.prakhar@bharatividyapeeth.edu.
[‖] Corresponding Author's Email: mohitdayal.md@gmail.com.

In: Blockchain and EHR
Editors: Kavita Saini, Amar Kumar and J. N. Singh
ISBN: 979-8-89113-380-8
© 2024 Nova Science Publishers, Inc.

and developed nations are conducting research into the creation and implementation of an electronic voting system based on blockchain technology. This study examines how blockchain technology might be incorporated into electronic voting systems to enhance the voting process by solving issues with security and privacy. Additionally, within the context of the paper, a software sample built using blockchain technology is provided, illuminating the key features of working with data.

**Keywords**: E-Voting, blockchain, voters, voting system, security, hyper ledger innovative technologies

## Introduction

Any human society's ability to function depends on its ability to vote. The success of nations and governments in the future depends on the resolution of significant economic, social, industrial, and political concerns. Because of this, the voting process must be simple, effective, as well as secure. Public concerns were once settled by a small group of people by raising their hands or tossing a predetermined object into an urn. The voting procedures have changed along with the advancement of society and the growth of the population living in the states. Voting booths, ballot boxes, and polling places all appeared as they became more accessible and transparent. Millions of people's opinions might now be registered and taken into account, thanks to these improvements [1, 2]. The risk of fake ballots and fake voting results, social pressure on voters, and the enormous expense of organizing elections (the 2018 presidential elections in the Russian Federation cost around $ 250 million) are all serious negatives of such a system.

The use of digital electronic voting in addition to or instead of traditional voting using paper ballots is appropriate today.

The switch to electronic voting allowed for a reduction in the expenditures associated with planning and conducting elections, but the security of this procedure is still an unresolved question. The most prevalent and significant issue voters in today's elections confront while using electronic voting is hacking or vote fabrication (Golubitchenko, 2019). This is caused by things like inadequate hardware security in electronic systems, mistakes made during software compilation, and flaws and vulnerabilities in the server component of the system. These flaws allow an attacker to download, change, or gain unauthorised access to confidential data that has been saved [2]. The security of electronic voting systems is a current concern because of this.

A wide range of digital systems can be made more secure, high-performing, and function better thanks to the development of technologies and solutions based on distributed ledgers, which can also address the issues these systems are prone to (Melanie, 2017). As a result, it is possible to create an electronic voting system using blockchain technology with a low chance that it will be hacked. As a result, it is appropriate and legal to employ secure distributed registers in electronic voting systems over the Internet.

By minimizing paperwork and using fewer human resources, such choices and agreements typically increase the number of voters, streamline the voting process, and lower expenses.

## Theoretical Foundation

In order to support Bitcoin, the first cryptocurrency, Satoshi Nakamoto invented the blockchain technology in 2008. A distributed, decentralised, and shared digital ledger that maintains a list of blocks might be referred to as blockchain technology [3]. Many suggestions have been made over time by many scholars to expand blockchain applications to non-financial areas such as electronic voting, used car markets, the pharmaceutical industry, etc.

## Features of Blockchain

### Decentralization

Conventional centralised transaction systems require that each transaction be verified by a single trusted third party (such as the central bank), which invariably leads to cost and performance bottlenecks at the central servers. In contrast to the centralised form, blockchain eliminates the necessity for third parties [3, 4]. blockchain uses consensus techniques to preserve data consistency across distributed networks.

### Immutability

This quality is crucial because it prevents easy modification of the transactions that are recorded in the ledger chain. Since it uses the hash function to create a secure chain, a transaction that has been committed and sent to the chain cannot be changed unless all nodes concur. This requires a significant amount of work.

**Distributed**

The same copy of the ledger is shared by every node in the network.

**Secure**

Blockchain employs a hash function, encryption, and decryption facilities, which make it secure.

**Open Source**

Anyone can download the source code, try to tweak it to create something new, publish it to the public, and profit from it.

## Applications of Blockchain

### Payment Methods

Considering that the first digital currency coins appeared and served as the evaluation, this industry may be entirely based on the blockchain [5].

### Voting

Everyone has heard about the Trump-Russia election controversy in the US. Therefore, none of that will occur if blockchain is employed in the voting process. As each node will be provided with unique information to ensure that the election process goes in the proper direction, a customised algorithm may be employed without the need for human intervention. Pharmaceutical Sector: Everyone is aware of the numerous problems this industry faces, including medication fraud [6]. Blockchain is consequently frequently used to track the manufacture of medications.

## Literature Survey

Before beginning my project, I conducted extensive study that involved reading several research articles that have been published in various books. When making a thorough reference to the literature during my investigation, I came up the following words: Web3.js, Metamask, Ganache, Truffle, Ethereum and ethers.

## Truffle

Truffle is a platform that makes it simple for designers to develop Ethereum-based blockchain-based apps. Using regional languages like JavaScript, designers are able to create and test trustworthy contracts as well as launch both public and private organizations. One outstanding and enticing aspect of Truffle is the command line tool. Several helpful commands are at our disposal, including assemble, move, repair, etc. The control centre is a quick and easy way to interface with the blockchain.

## Ethereum and Ethers

Scalable, programmable, secure, and decentralised are all features of Ethereum. It is the blockchain of choice for developers and businesses that are building technologies on top of it to transform several sectors and how we live our everyday lives. People all throughout the world will benefit from having a framework thanks to this. The only model that won't protect itself against hacking and closure is the glorified Ethereum one since no feature will have control over your personal data. Ether is used as a collateral or bond by the sender of a computer service and is a fix for the instalment problem. Because it doesn't need a third party to support or oversee the transaction, ether functions as a currency. Ether is not truly a digital money, though. It is frequently used as a fuel for apps that run on the Ethereum network.

## Web3.js

A visual user interface for the programme with a sizable JavaScript library is called Web3.js, and it enables programmers to accept smart contracts. Depending on the intricacy of the Divided Applications application, a designer may integrate sophisticated conclusions by creating dynamic Java projects or even become acquainted with their Dedicated application knowledge by creating intelligence-related Python projects. The JSON RPC conference connects this to our nationally distributed blockchain application. By using a Web3 even, one may without a certain link with everything immediately in the order line.

## MetaMask

A basic cryptocurrency wallet is MetaMask. Designers can benefit from using MetaMask to test and assess dApp transactions. Successful collaboration between MetaMask and a nearby blockchain operating engine. Copy your localhost hole from the Truffle console, then paste it into a system extension-accessible custom RPC. Truffle and MetaMask can effectively import records. The Ethereum biological system has received remarkable and well-known support from MetaMask [7]. There is no question that developers can swap between blockchains. When a client accesses a DApp, MetaMask serves as a blockchain intermediary. Furthermore, the MetaMask GUI is incredibly simple to use. It reliably establishes a connection between the client and the blockchain.

The client is informed by MetaMask to support the exchange. For connecting to a blockchain, a client may pay this and other trades in cryptocurrency fees. The Ethereum biological system has received fantastic and well-known support from MetaMask. There is no doubt that developers can swap between blockchains.

When a client accesses a dApp, MetaMask functions as a blockchain intermediary. The GUI for MetaMask is also very simple to use. It continually links a client to the blockchain. A client is prompted by MetaMask to support an exchange [8]. This exchange is only an occasional fee that a client might incur in cryptocurrency to link to the blockchain.

## Ganache

Programs called Ethereum smart contracts are run inside the context of transactions on the Ethereum blockchain.

The Truffle Suite, a group of engineering tools that let users test smart contracts locally and replicate blockchain circumstances, includes Ethereum Ganache. A local in-memory blockchain for testing and enhancement is called Ethereum Ganache.

## E-Voting Using Blockchain

With several operational uses, blockchain is emerging as a significant new feature. While distributed applications, including text sharing, have existed before the beginning of the Web, their usage in safe and reliable trade dates back to that year [8]. Since then, as Bitcoin has grown in popularity, more people and businesses are becoming aware of the advantages that blockchain innovation has to offer.

The voting booth is one of the most recent yet most innovative blockchain uses. Email voting will soon become the norm in regular circumstances.

Electronic voting will enhance the democratic election process by making it quicker, easier, and less expensive, while also increasing the number of voters and supporting systems that need voters to cast their ballots. Electronic voting, according to many experts in the area, needs high-tech security measures, which can only be offered by blockchain technology, which has its own distribution environment and prevents voter interference.

## Online Voting System Advantages

In my system I have a good scalability and this can applied to any voting system in the world. In my system the admin only add voters, candidates, and create the election day without interfering in the voters or the results. our system is performing well as the time it needs to performed a transaction is less. The proposed system will reduce election costs by 90%, as there will be no need to do all of the election preparation work that was previously required when voting by paper and pin.

## Methodologies

I take into account current and previous electronic voting frameworks as I implement a blockchain-enabled electronic democracy framework. Different cycles for describing occupations and evaluating structures, security, and legal matters should be taken into consideration [9]. The system that was created has been given the name "EVOTE," and will always be referred to by that name in this work. It attempts to offer a real-time online voting tool that may be used to any amount of selection. It will endeavor to improve elections at the national level as well as those that take place in towns, suburbs, and organisations. Additionally, we made an effort to keep the programme as straightforward as possible so that it would run on outdated systems like those found in rural areas. I defined the election in our electoral system as a smart contract. Therefore, in my network, a decision is made by participating nodes in accord. Furthermore, a wise contract will specify each role participant, the election procedure, and the terms and circumstances applicable to the election.

Each participant needs to be assigned to a certain role. Most people are capable of receiving either the same job or a different role.

### Administrators

All electoral procedures will be supervised by administrators. They may be assigned imaginative tasks to demonstrate the validity of the election, as well as the votes' impact on the computation, close selection, and revelation of outcomes. He will be able to create elections thanks to this admin function. Only once the election has been created by the admin may a user cast their vote. Between the start date and the finish date, users can cast ballots.

### Voters

A voter is a key participant in an election who casts a ballot. Voters can upload their ballots, self-certify, and confirm their eligibility. They can cast a ballot and then verify it.

## Election Process

The arrangement of smart contracts that are enabled into the blockchain is used to conduct the voting process. The smart contracts are accurately described as being for jobs that are described to the organization's members.

The administrators have the authority to start the election, add candidates, check the list of registered candidates, and call it to a close. The voting ballots can also be created by administrators using decentralized software. The voters' constituencies and candidates can also be specified by an admin. The ballot is created via the smart contract and deployed into the blockchain.

This voting method consists of several steps. With the aid of a private key that will be produced on the administrator server, the voter may also register via the registration tab. The voter can register himself and enable gas transactions through the Metamask platform with the use of that private key [9]. The administrator must pay ethers, or gas, to verify each voter. The voter identification number and name submitted at the time of pre-registration are verified. An individual voter interacts with the secret ballot when casting their ballot.

When the smart contract and blockchain communicate, the vote is added if the code matches. Once a person has cast a ballot, they are not permitted to do so again. This is so that each person may only use the created private key once. The winner's declaration once the election is over is essential. Since everything is done digitally, the administrator closes the polls after counting all the votes that were cast for a particular candidate. Each voter may now access the website's results on their personal computers.

## Architecture

Admin. will launch/deploy the system on a blockchain network (EVM), establish a voting instance, build an election instance, and start the election with all of the election's data filled in (including candidates for people to vote on and his own detail). Below are the few tables including Table 1, shows the structure of Admin table, Table 2 shows the structure of Election information, Table 3 and Table 4 shows the candidate data and list of candidates respectively.

**Table 1. About Admin**

| Full Name | Bankuri |
|---|---|
| Last Name | Singal |
| Email | rohtak.bankuri123@gmail.com |
| Job Title | Admin |

**Table 2. About Election**

| Election Title | College Election |
|---|---|
| Organization Name | BVCOE |

**Table 3. Add Candidate**

| Header |
|---|
| Slogan |

**Table 4. List of Candidates**

|   | Header | Slogan |
|---|---|---|
| 0. | Yush | Save Earth Save Life |
| 1. | Vaansi | Earth Day – Everyday |
| 2. | Krrishu | No Earth No Birth |
| 3. | Shivom | Redisco Yourself |

The potential voters then sign up to vote on the same blockchain network by connecting to it.

Voter's Registered Information of three different users is shown below Table 5, Table 6 and Table 7.

**Table 5. Voter-1 Registered Information**

| Account Address | 0x7BcFb316B77B7e0BdA150a38C78397A43A89ed13 |
|---|---|
| Name | Shivom |
| Phone | 1287452235 |
| Voted | False |
| Verification | False |
| Registered | True |

Online Voting System on a Secure Platform 55

**Table 6.** Voter-2 Registered Information

| Account Address | 0x21aFDc52c96056348851c3bf6fa3C07179E19D4a |
|---|---|
| Name | Ponuma |
| Phone | 7859641236 |
| Voted | False |
| Verification | False |
| Registered | True |

**Table 7.** Voter-3 Registered Information

| Account Address | 0x15787c70527C16c6F80E8893E3F7c1E21f8129E3 |
|---|---|
| Name | Sulesas |
| Phone | 1296541235 |
| Voted | False |
| Verification | False |
| Registered | True |

After properly registering, users' information is delivered to or shown on the admins' panel (i.e., verification page). The administrator will next verify that the registration data, including the name and phone number of the blockchain account, is accurate and matches his records. If so, the administrator gives the registered user the go-ahead to participate in the election and cast their vote [10, 11]. After receiving admin clearance, the registered user (voter) casts their ballot for the desired candidate (from the voting page).

Depending on the size of the election, the administration stops the election after a while [12]. The voting is then closed, and the results are shown, with the winner's name at the top of the results page as shown in Table 8.

Figure 1 depicts the overall architecture online voting system.

**Table 8.** Result Page

| 0. | Yash | 2 |
|---|---|---|
| 1. | Vansh | 0 |
| 2. | Krrish | 1 |
| 3. | Shiv | 0 |

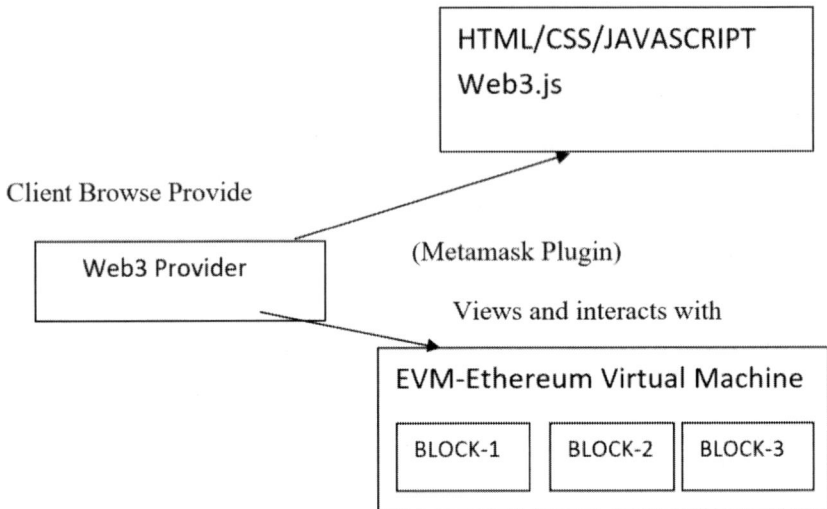

**Figure 1.** Architecture.

## Conclusion

At this point, near the end of this chapter, I can assume that I have read numerous research papers about creating an electronic democratic framework using blockchain technology and that I have ultimately discovered that there are numerous approaches to dealing with create an electronic democratic framework with the aid of square chain technology. Additionally, I have noted that in order to do my duty, I need to be aware of various developments like Ethereum and truffle.

## References

[1] Al-Maaitah, S., Mohammad Qatawneh, Abdullah Quzmar. E-Voting System Based on Blockchain Technology: A Survey. *2021 International Conference on Information Technology (ICIT)*.

[2] Qatawneh, M., Wesam Almobaideen, Orieb AbuAlghanam (2020). Challenges of Blockchain Technology in Context Internet of Things: A Survey. *International Journal of Computer Applications*, Vol. 175.

[3] Afif Monrat, A., Olov Schelen, and Karl Andersson (August 19, 2019). A Survey of Blockchain from the Perspectives of Applications, Challenges, and Opportunities. *Digital Object Identifier* https://doi.org/10.1109/ACCESS.2019.293609.

[4] Dagher, Gaby G., Marella, Praneeth Babu, Milojkovic, Matea, and Mohler Jordan (2018, January). BroncoVote: Secure Voting System Using Ethereum's Blockchain. *In the 4th International Conference on Information Systems Security and Privacy (ICISSP)*, 96-107.

[5] Ahmada, S., Siti Alida John Bt Abdullahb and Rozita Bt Arshadc. (2015). Issues and Challenges of Transition to e-Voting Technology in Nigeria. *Public Policy and Administration Research* ISSN 2224-5731(Paper) ISSN 2225-0972(Online) Vol. 5, No. 4, 2015

[6] Asassfeh, M. R., Qatawneh, M., & AL-Azzeh, F. M. (2018). Performance evaluation of blowfish algorithm on supercomputer iman1. *International Journal of Computer Networks & Communications* (IJCNC), 10(2).

[7] Poniszewska-Marańda, A., Michał Pawlak and Jakub Guziur (2020. Auditable blockchain voting system – the blockchain technology toward the electronic voting process. *Int. J. Web and Grid Services*, Vol. 16, No. 1, 2020.

[8] Karneedi, K., (2020). *E-Voting using Blockchain.* https://doi.org/10.13140/RG.2.2.29954.71360.

[9] Jayapal, C. & Sekar, Navin & Sekar, Raghul & Suresh, Rajkumar. (2020). *Secured Voting Using Blockchain.* 177-184. https://doi.org/10.1109/ICCCA49541.2020.9250859.

[10] Prajapati, A. & Reddy, Vandana. (2020). *Online Voting System Using Blockchain.* https://doi.org/10.1007/978-981-15-5394_67.

[11] Febriyanto, E. & Triyono, & Rahayu, Nina & Pangaribuan, Kelvin & Sunarya, Po. (2020). *Using Blockchain Data Security Management for E-Voting Systems* 1-4. https://doi.org/10.1109/CITSM50537.2020.9268847.

[12] Saini, K., Kumari, K. and Sagar, S., 2021. Blockchain Securing Drug Supply Chain : Combating counterfeits. In *Blockchain and IoT Integration* (pp. 77-88). Auerbach Publications.

## Chapter 5

# Enhancing Data Storage Security Using Web3 and Cryptography

**Bishal Kumar**[*]
**Janhavi Soni**
**Sudeep Singh Yadav**
**and J. N. Singh**
School of Computing Science and Engineering, Galgotias University,
Greater Noida, India

## Abstract

Concern over people's privacy is growing because of the rapid advancement of technology based on big data and information. Although there isn't a clear definition of what privacy is, various viewpoints generally take into account people's respect, autonomy, and self-determination as well as how they should be protected from unreasonable intrusions into their privacy, even by government or commercial institutions. In the context of technical information, privacy can be characterized as the right of individuals to manage the use of about the collection, handling, storing, and use of their personal information). Web applications have been governed by centralized providers for a significant portion of the history of the Internet. The logic and data of the program are controlled by these suppliers, who have complete control over editing and erasing it. Web3 distributes web applications through a Peer-to-Peer (P2P) network of linked nodes. Data cannot be deleted or changed without the network's agreement, data is always visible to all nodes, and there is no central authority or controller. The purpose of the

---

[*] Corresponding Author's Email: singhbishalkumarsingh@gmail.com.

In: Blockchain and EHR
Editors: Kavita Saini, Amar Kumar and J. N. Singh
ISBN: 979-8-89113-380-8
© 2024 Nova Science Publishers, Inc.

suggested study is to use web3 (which includes blockchain) and cryptography to increase the security of people's data. We'll be employing ASE to strengthen the security of our system and make it impenetrable to hackers as part of architectural research. Blockchain serves as a distributed ledger that makes it possible for smart contracts to efficiently aggregate data. ASE will be utilized on the top. Data encryption enables processes for private aggregation. To support the theoretical description, a suggested implementation, potential applications, and a performance study are offered.

**Keywords:** blockchain, Web3, cryptography, AES (advanced encryption standard), P2P(peer-to-peer), aggregation, decentralization

## Introduction

Cloud storage is one of the leading options to store massive data, however, the centralized storage approach of cloud computing is not secure, as the entire data remains at the mercy of the centralized data store provider. It can be leaked or destroyed, or any mishap can happen to the data.

As the world is changing rapidly, similarly the Web is changing. In the 1990s, the web accessible to humans was WEB1.0, which could only let the user consume data. Later on, in the $21^{st}$ century, technology upgraded, and the mass got access to WEB2.0, which enabled humans not only to consume but write their data as well, or send data through the web. Currently, we are using WEB2.0. The major problem in this version of the web is that all the data is controlled by a central body or a server, which is owned by a particular entity, which makes it more prudent to data leaks and increases the concerns about data privacy.

Now the next boom is WEB3.0. which uses blockchain as a medium to work, reducing the factor of data loss or leaks, as blockchain is fundamentally unalterable making them more secure for data storage. Blockchain is a decentralized cloud storage system that ensures data security. Any computing node connected to the internet can join and form peers' network thereby maximizing resource utilization. Blockchain is a distributed peer-to-peer system where each node in the network stores a copy of the blockchain thus making it immutable.

In the chapter, a brief discussion is made right from the beginning of the internet and the present day. Especially focusing on the security threats of WEB 2.0 and the technologies in web 3.0 for encountering security issues.

Besides, a superior methodology has likewise been uncovered which can help in improving data storage security utilizing web3 and cryptography.
The chapter also uncovers the technical depth of the entire methodology. Along with the tools and the technologies being used. It not only educates but also tries to enhance the way by which users store his/her sensitive information on the blockchain, with the help of an easy-to-use architecture. Making it secure and easily accessible all over the internet.

This methodology can be used for research purposes as well, there is very fewer research available on the internet about the security enhancement of data that is being stored on the blockchain using cryptography. By reading the chapter the user can get in-depth information required for storing data more securely on the web.

## Background

### Time before the Internet

The time before the internet was not very same as the way we live today. The internet has revolutionized the way we access information and communicate with others and not only this, but it also has a diverse range of effects on our daily habits but what was life like before the invention of the internet? In the past people had to rely on other methods to access information and communicate with others this could include reading books or magazines watching television or movies listening to the radio or making phone calls for many people these were the primary sources of information and entertainment [1].

Researching a topic typically involved going to a library or bookstore to find books or other resources on the subject this could be a time-consuming and sometimes frustrating process as libraries and bookstores may not always have the specific information you were looking for.

In terms of communication people used a variety of methods to stay in touch with others this could include sending letters through the mail making phone calls or using fax machines to send documents these methods of communication were generally slower than what we have today with the internet as it could take days or even weeks for a letter to be delivered and phone calls and faxes were often expensive overall life before the internet was generally slower-paced and more reliant on traditional forms of communication and information-gathering people had to be more patient and resourceful to access the information and connect with others that they needed.

Despite these challenges, there were also some benefits to life before the internet for example people may have spent more time face-to-face with others rather than communicating through screens they may have also had more time to engage in hobbies and other activities as they didn't have the same level of access to a constant stream of information and distractions in conclusion life before the internet was very different from the way we live today.

The Internet has greatly changed the way we access information and communicate with others making it easier and more convenient to connect with people and access a vast amount of information however there were also some benefits to life before the internet such as more face-to-face interaction and time for hobbies and other activities.

**Rapid Changing Environment of the Internet around Us**

There have been numerous significant achievements in the turn of events and advancement of the web since its commencement [2][3]. Here is a rundown of probably the main achievements, in the field of the internet which clearly explains the transition of the web:

- 1969: The main web association is laid out between PCs at UCLA and the Stanford Exploration Organization. This was the initial occasion when PCs in various areas had the option to speak with one another utilizing the web.
- 1971: The primary email is sent. Beam Tomlinson, a PC engineer, sent the primary email utilizing the ARPANET organization, the forerunner to the web.
- 1973: The primary global web association is laid out between the US and the Assembled Realm. This was a significant achievement in the globalization of the web and made it ready for worldwide correspondence and joint effort.
- 1983: The Space Name Framework (DNS) is presented, which permits web clients to get to sites utilizing simple to-recollect area names rather than long, confounded IP addresses.
- 1989: The main form of the Internet, created by Tim Berners-Lee, is presented. This made it feasible for individuals to access and share data on the web utilizing an internet browser.

- 1993: The principal web search tool, Archie, is made. This permitted clients to scan the web for explicit data and made it more straightforward to find sites and assets on the web.
- 1995: The primary internet shopping website, Amazon, is sent off. This was a significant achievement in the development of web-based business and made ready for the multiplication of internet shopping stages.
- 1996: The primary online entertainment stage, Six Degrees, is sent off. This permitted clients to interface with one another on the web and started the development of virtual entertainment stages like Facebook, Twitter, and Instagram.
- 1997: Google is established, ultimately turning into the prevailing web crawler and quite possibly the best organization on the planet.
- 1998: The principal texting stage, ICQ, is sent off. This reformed the manner in which individuals conveyed on the web and made ready for well-known informing applications like WhatsApp and Skype.
- 2002: The primary internet web-based stage, Netflix, is sent off. This altered the manner in which individuals consumed media and prepared for the expansion of streaming stages like Hulu and Disney+.
- 2004: Facebook is sent off, in the end turning into the biggest online entertainment stage on the planet.
- 2007: The first cell phone, the iPhone, is presented. This upset the manner in which individuals got to the web and started the development of versatile web utilization.
- 2010: The main tablet PC, the iPad, is presented. This significantly had an impact on the manner in which individuals involved the web and prepared for the expansion of tablet gadgets.
- 2014: The principal augmented reality headset, the Oculus Fracture, is presented. This started the development of augmented reality innovation and opened up additional opportunities for web clients.
- 2016: The primary business self-driving vehicle is presented. This undeniably a significant achievement in the improvement of independent vehicles and opened up additional opportunities for web associated transportation.
- 2018: The European Association presents the Overall Information Insurance Guideline (GDPR), which controls the assortment and utilization of individual information on the web.

- 2020: The Coronavirus pandemic prompts a huge expansion in remote work and web based picking up, prompting a flood in web utilization and the development of new advances like virtual gatherings and online classes.

## Web Versions and Divisions Helpful in Understanding the Current Topic

The World Wide Web (WWW or Web) is a vast network of interconnected documents and other resources, linked by hyperlinks and URLs. It allows users to access and share information using a web browser. Since its inception, the Web has undergone many changes and updates, with new versions being released periodically to improve its functionality and capabilities. Here is a brief overview of the major versions of the Web, along with their advantages and disadvantages:

### Web 1.0
This was the first version of the Web, introduced in 1989 by Tim Berners-Lee. It was a static, read-only platform that allowed users to access and view information, but not to interact with it or share it. The advantages of Web 1.0 included its simplicity and ease of use, as well as the fact that it made it possible for people to access and share information on a global scale. Disadvantages included the lack of interactivity and the inability to easily update or change information.

### Web 2.0
This version of the Web, introduced in the early 2000s, focused on the concept of Web 2.0, which refers to the ability for users to interact with and contribute to the Web. It introduced new technologies like blogs, social media platforms, and wikis, which allowed users to create and share their content. The advantages of Web 2.0 included increased interactivity and user-generated content, as well as the ability to easily connect and collaborate with others. Disadvantages included the potential for misinformation and the need for users to have a certain level of technical proficiency to fully utilize the new features [4].

## Web 3.0

This version of the Web, also known as the Semantic Web, focuses on the idea of using machine-readable data to enable computers to understand and interpret the meaning of information on the Web. It uses technologies like artificial intelligence, natural language processing, and machine learning to create a more intelligent and intuitive Web experience. Advantages of Web 3.0 include the potential for more personalized and targeted content, as well as the ability to automate and streamline certain tasks. Disadvantages include the potential for privacy concerns and the need for advanced technology and infrastructure to fully utilize the new features [5][6].

## Web 4.0

This version of the Web, also known as the Internet of Things (IoT), focuses on the integration of the Web with physical devices and objects. It allows these devices to communicate with each other and the internet, creating a network of connected devices that can share data and perform tasks automatically. The advantages of Web 4.0 include the potential for increased efficiency and automation, as well as the ability to gather and analyze large amounts of data. Disadvantages include the potential for security and privacy concerns, as well as the need for advanced technology and infrastructure to fully utilize the new features.

## Web 5.0

This is an emerging version of the Web that is still being developed and is not yet widely available. It is expected to focus on the integration of virtual and augmented reality technology with the Web, creating a more immersive and interactive experience for users. The advantages of Web 5.0 include the potential for more immersive and interactive content, as well as the ability to create new types of experiences and applications. Disadvantages include the potential for technical challenges and the need for advanced technology and infrastructure to fully utilize the new features.

Overall, each version of the Web has brought its advantages and disadvantages, and the evolution of the Web has been shaped by the needs and preferences of its users. As the Internet proceeds to develop and new advancements arise, we will probably see significantly more changes and enhancements to the manner in which we access and use it.

**Issues in WEB 2.0**

Web 2.0 refers to the ability for users to interact with and contribute to the Web. It introduced new technologies like blogs, social media platforms, and wikis, which allow users to create and share their own content. While these technologies have greatly enhanced the interactivity and user-generated content of the Web, they have also introduced new security concerns [7]. Some of the major security issues in Web 2.0 include:

- *Misinformation*: With the ability for anyone to create and share content on the Web, there is a risk of misinformation being spread. This can be particularly problematic on social media platforms, where misinformation can spread quickly and cause harm.
- *Phishing attacks*: Web 2.0 technologies like social media and email have made it easier for attackers to impersonate legitimate websites or individuals in order to trick users into giving away sensitive information, such as login credentials or financial information.
- *Privacy concerns*: Web 2.0 technologies often collect and use personal data in order to provide targeted content and ads. However, this can raise concerns about the protection of users' privacy and the potential for this data to be misused.
- *Malware*: Web 2.0 technologies like blogs and social media can be used to spread malware, which can infect users' devices and compromise their security.
- *Cyberbullying*: Web 2.0 technologies like social media and messaging apps can be used to bully or harass others online, which can have serious consequences for the victims.

To address these security issues, it is important for users to be aware of the risks and take steps to protect themselves. These massive security flaws in this form of the web gave rise to a newer and more robust form of the web "THE WEB 3.0".

**WEB 3.0 "The Saviour of WEB 2.0" Rectifying the Security Issues in Web 2.0**

Web 3.0 (see Figure 1), otherwise called the Semantic Web, is an arising rendition of the Internet that spotlights on utilizing machine-comprehensible information to empower PCs to comprehend and decipher the significance of data Online. It utilizes technologies like blockchain, and cryptography to create a more intelligent and intuitive Web experience.

Blockchain is a distributed ledger technology that allows multiple parties to securely record and verify transactions without the need for a central authority. It is often associated with the use of cryptocurrencies like Bitcoin, but it has many other potential applications as well.

One way that blockchain could potentially address some of the security issues in Web 2.0 is by providing a secure and transparent platform for recording and verifying transactions and other types of data. For example, it could be used to verify the authenticity of the information or the identity of individuals, helping to prevent the spread of misinformation or the occurrence of phishing attacks.

Blockchain could also potentially address privacy concerns by providing a secure and decentralized platform for storing and accessing personal data. Instead of having a central authority controlling and potentially misusing personal data, the decentralized nature of blockchain could allow individuals to have more control over their own data and how it is used.

Overall, the potential for blockchain to provide a secure and transparent platform for recording and verifying transactions and other types of data could make it a useful tool for addressing security issues in Web 2.0. However, it is important to note that blockchain is still a relatively new and evolving technology, and it is not yet clear how it will be used and integrated into the Web in the future.

Furthermore, Web 3.0 could potentially address some of the security issues in Web 2.0 by using artificial intelligence and machine learning to identify and flag misinformation or malicious content. For example, AI algorithms could be used to analyze the veracity of the information or the intentions of a post or message, and alert users or platform administrators if there are any concerns. This could help to mitigate the spread of misinformation and prevent phishing attacks or other malicious activity.

Web 3.0 could also potentially address privacy concerns by using AI and machine learning to better understand and protect users' data. For example, AI algorithms could be used to analyze data usage patterns and identify any potential privacy violations and alert users or administrators if there are any concerns. This could help to ensure that personal data is used responsibly and only for the purposes for which it was intended.

Overall, the potential for Web 3.0 to use advanced technologies like blockchain, cryptography, AI, and machine learning to improve security and address issues like misinformation and privacy concerns could make it a more secure and trustworthy platform for users.

In recent times there has been tremendous development in technologies that can be used to leverage the advantages of blockchain using an easy-to-use interface that is easily integrable with current technology helping in making the upcoming applications more decentralized and more secure.

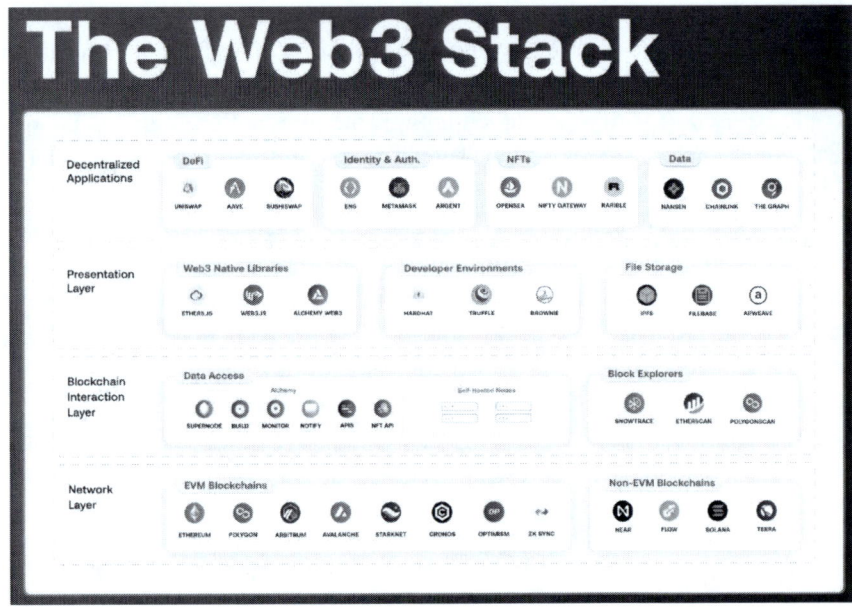

**Figure 1.** Advancement in Tools and Technologies Used in Web 3.

## Proposed Work

Cloud storage is one of the leading options to store massive data, however, the centralized storage approach of cloud computing is not secure, as the entire data remains at the mercy of the centralized data store provider. It can be leaked or destroyed, or any mishap can happen to the data.

As the world is changing rapidly, similarly the Web is changing. In the 1990s, the web accessible to humans was WEB1.0, which could only let the user consume data. Later on, in the 21st century, technology upgraded, and the mass got access to WEB2.0, which enabled humans not only to consume but write their own data as well or send data through the web.

Currently, we are using WEB2.0. The major problem in this version of the web is that all the data is controlled by a central body or a server, which is owned by a particular entity, which makes it more prudent to data leaks and increases the concerns about data privacy.

Now the next boom is WEB3.0. which uses blockchain as a medium to work, reducing the factor of data loss or leaks, as blockchain is fundamentally unalterable making them more secure for data storage. Any computing node connected to the internet can join and form peers' network thereby maximizing resource utilization. Blockchain is a distributed peer-to-peer system where each node in the network stores a copy of the blockchain thus making it immutable.

Here the focus is on identity information, which is more crucial and needs much protection, it is somehow similar to decentralized identity. But not in all aspects. Decentralized identity refers to a system of identity management that is not controlled by any single entity, but rather is distributed and decentralized as shown in Figure 2. This type of identity management has several benefits over traditional, centralized systems.

One key benefit is increased privacy and control for the individual. In a centralized system, an individual's identity is often stored in a central database that is managed by a single entity, such as a government agency or a private company. This central database can be a target for hackers, and the information it contains can be accessed and used by the entity controlling the database without the individual's consent.

In a decentralized identity system, on the other hand, an individual's identity is stored on a decentralized network, such as a blockchain. This means that the individual has more control over their own identity, as they are able to manage it themselves rather than relying on a central authority. Additionally, decentralized systems are generally more secure, as they are more resistant to tampering and hacking than centralized systems.

Another benefit of decentralized identity is increased interoperability. In a centralized system, different organizations often have their own separate systems for identity management, which can lead to problems when trying to exchange information or verify identities. With a decentralized system, on the other hand, different organizations can use a common platform for identity management, which makes it easier to exchange information and verify identities.

Overall, decentralized identity systems offer a number of benefits over centralized systems, including increased privacy, control, and interoperability [8][9].

At this point, it's important to understand the methodologies available for the storage of the Identity information of a user on blockchain [10].

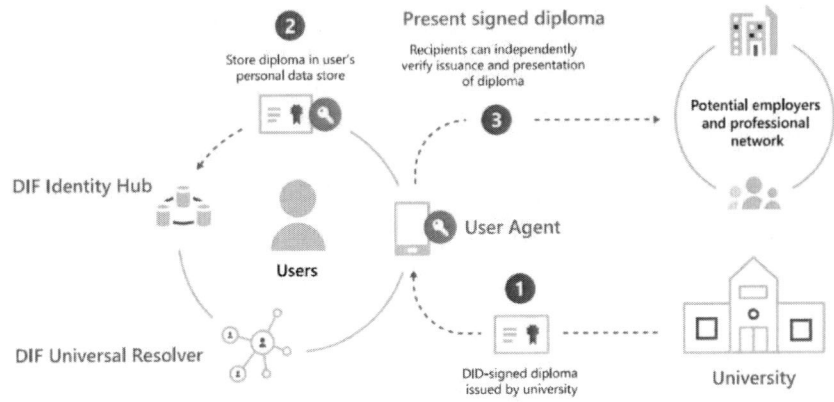

**Figure 2.** Working of Decentralized Identity.

## The Two Ways to Store Data on Blockchain

*(a) Storing Data on Chain*
On-chain describes verifiable events or exchanges that occur immediately on the blockchain. In this scenario, the user directly uploads files to a blockchain also counts as an on-chain activity.

But Large file storage on the blockchain can be quite expensive. A gigabyte of storage on the blockchain costs about $100 USD, which is 500 times more expensive than conventional storage, according to IBM's "Storage Needs for Blockchain Technology - Point of View document".

In addition to being costly, storing a lot of files on a blockchain might cause access latency (the amount of time it takes to upload/download files from the blockchain) to increase. Low latency is needed for file storage to enable quick access. But when latency increases because of large files, the blockchain system's performance may suffer, and maintenance may become exceedingly challenging.

Non-transactional data including files, contracts, documents, PDFs, and personal information shouldn't be kept on the blockchain directly; instead, it should be kept off-chain.

## (b) Storing Data Off-Chain

Off-chain refers to operations or exchanges that take place apart from the blockchain. A file that is not immediately posted to the blockchain is referred to in this sense as an off-chain asset. Since it is not a good idea to store non-transactional data, the file is uploaded to a different server or database (such as IPFS, MongoDB, Oracle, etc.), and the blockchain will store the created Hash ID as metadata.

From the above discussion, it is very clear that data should be preferred to be stored off-chain in order to prevent cost inflation and reduce latency. Hence, IPFS can be used for data storage. Whereas blockchain serves as a medium to store the CID of the stored data on IPFS and further for sharing the identity data of the user with another user.

This in turn increases the redundancy of the system and furthermore, the CID can be encrypted by the private key of the user in demand of the data. And then can be sent using blockchain in its metadata.

The current state of research on how these technologies can be used to improve the security of data storage has been done. Web3 refers to the third generation of the World Wide Web, which is focused on leveraging decentralized technologies such as blockchain and peer-to-peer networks to enable new applications and services. Cryptography is the practice of secure communication, which involves the use of mathematical techniques to encode and decode data.

Research in this area has focused on using web3 technologies such as blockchain and decentralized storage systems to improve the security and privacy of data storage. For example, blockchain technology can be used to create tamper-evident, decentralized databases that can store sensitive data in a secure and transparent manner. Decentralized storage systems, such as Inter-Planetary File Systems (IPFS), can be used to store data in a distributed manner, making it more resilient to attacks and failures.

Cryptography has also been used to enhance the security of data storage by enabling secure communication and data protection. For example, encryption algorithms can be used to protect data from unauthorized access, and digital signatures can be used to verify the authenticity of data.

Overall, the use of web3 technologies and cryptography has the potential to significantly enhance the security and privacy of data storage, making it more difficult for data to be accessed or altered without permission. Further research is needed to explore the full potential of these technologies and to develop best practices for their use in data storage.

Currently, there seem to be no or very less solutions available for the storage of decentralized identity. Hence, this raises a problem statement. In order to counter this problem an advanced decentralized application has been formulated, which is capable of storing identity information onto blockchain, while maintaining the security of data while in communicating the information [11].

## Technical Background

As discussed earlier it is very clear that data should be stored off-chain. Hence, IPFS is being used for data storage.

Interplanetary File System (IPFS) is a decentralized, peer-to-peer file-sharing network that allows users to store and share files in a distributed manner, rather than relying on a central server. IPFS can be used to store a variety of types of information, including identity information [12].

Storing identity information on Interplanetary File System (IPFS) and using blockchain technology to manage access to that information is a decentralized and secure way to manage identity. Here is how it could be done:

1. A user creates a file containing their identity information and adds it to the IPFS network. The file is assigned a unique hash, which is used to identify it on the network.
2. The user creates a smart contract on a blockchain platform, such as Ethereum, that defines the conditions under which the identity information can be accessed. The smart contract includes the **hash** of the identity file on IPFS as well as the **public key** of the user who owns the identity information.
3. Other users who want to access the identity information can send a request to the smart contract, specifying the conditions under which they want to access the information. If the conditions are met, the smart contract retrieves the identity file from IPFS using the hash and sends it to the requesting user. Here in case if the requestee provides his/her public key then the smart contract encrypts the hash with the public key of the requestee and then sends it to him/her.
4. The requesting user can then access the identity information contained in the file by decrypting the hash received by his private key.

Enhancing Data Storage Security Using Web3 and Cryptography 73

This process allows the user to have control over their own identity information and to specify the conditions under which it can be accessed. It also provides a secure and transparent way for other users to access the information, as the access is mediated by the smart contract on the blockchain.

Overall, using IPFS and blockchain technology together allows for a decentralized, secure, and transparent way to manage and access identity information.

**For Storing User's Data (see Figure 3)**

- Authentication/Authorization
- Wallet Login in the browser
- Storage on IPFS
- Retrieval of unique Hash
- Storage of the Hash into decentralized application's database (e.g.: MongoDB)

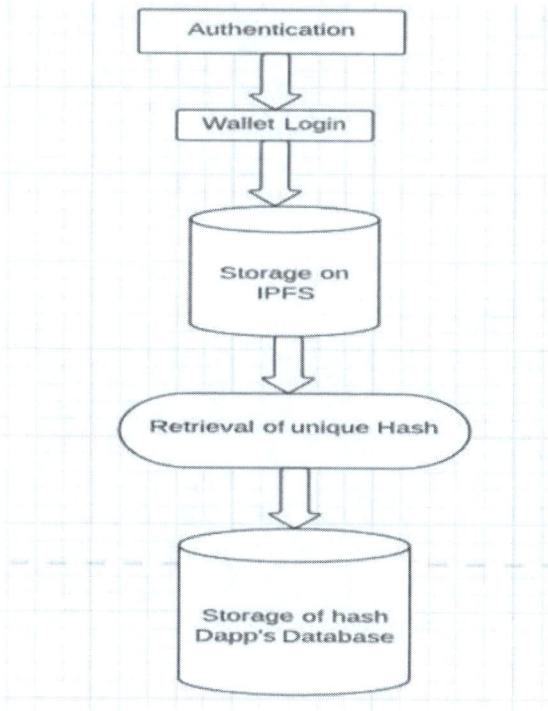

**Figure 3.** For Storing User Data Accessing.

## The Identity Information (see Figure 4)

- Logging in to the application
- MetaMask Wallet Login in the browser
- Request the required data with own public key
- The smart contract executes and encrypts the required CID with the public key provided
- Executes the transaction in the blockchain registry (Ethereum registry)
- The user has access to the required data in the form of an encrypted CID. This encrypted CID can only be decrypted using the private key of the user
- The user uses his/her private key to decrypt the CID and retrieves the required information from IPFS

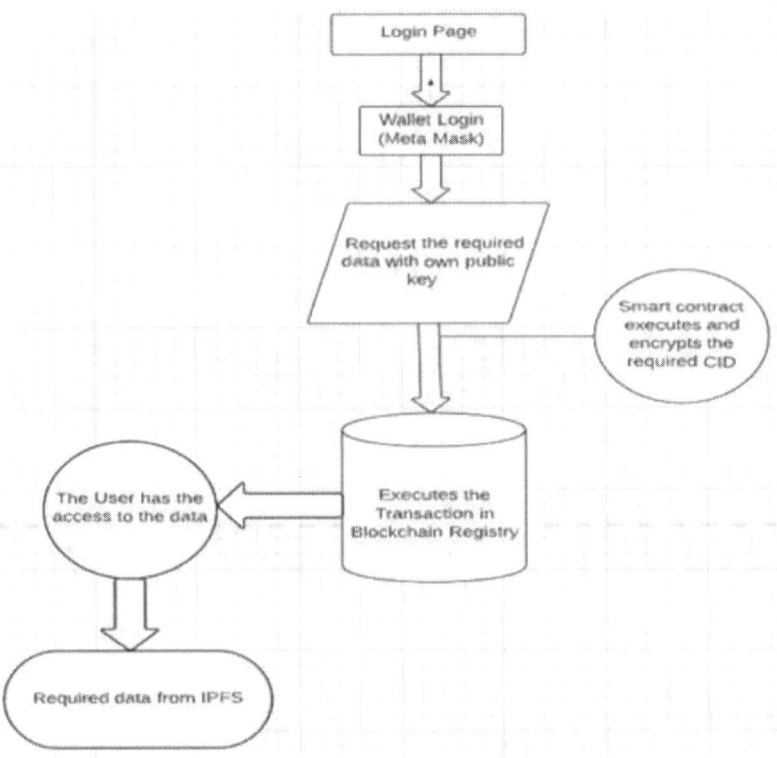

**Figure 4.** Accessing Identity Information.

## Understanding Working of Technologies Involved in Web 3.0

### Blockchain

Blockchain is a distributed ledger technology that allows multiple parties to securely record and verify transactions without the need for a central authority. It is often associated with the use of cryptocurrencies like Bitcoin, but it has many other potential applications as well.

At its core, a blockchain is a decentralized database that consists of a series of blocks, each of which contains a record of multiple transactions. These blocks are linked together in a chain using cryptographic techniques, which makes it difficult for anyone to alter or delete the data within them.

Each block in a blockchain contains a number of transactions, as well as a unique code called a "hash" that identifies the block and links it to the previous block in the chain. The hash of a block is created using the data within the block and the hash of the previous block, which ensures that any changes to the data in a block will result in a different hash value. This makes it virtually impossible to alter the data within a block without being detected [13].

In order to add a new block to a blockchain, the transactions within it must be verified by a network of computers, known as nodes. These nodes work together to validate the transactions and ensure that they are accurate and legitimate. Once a block has been validated, it is added to the end of the chain and becomes a permanent part of the blockchain.

One of the key features of a blockchain is its decentralized nature, which means that it is not controlled by a single authority or organization. Instead, it is maintained by a network of computers that work together to validate and record transactions. This makes it a secure and transparent platform for recording and verifying transactions and other types of data.

There are many different types of blockchain, each with its own characteristics and uses. Some of the most well-known types of blockchain include:

- *Public blockchain*: These are open and decentralized blockchain that anyone can participate in. Examples include Bitcoin and Ethereum.
- *Private blockchain*: These are closed and centralized blockchain that are only accessible to a specific group of individuals or organizations. They are often used by businesses to track and verify internal transactions.

- *Hybrid blockchain*: These are blockchain that combine elements of both public and private blockchain. They are often used to create a balance between security and accessibility.
- Blockchain has the potential to revolutionize a wide range of industries and applications, from financial services and supply chain management to healthcare and voting systems. Some of the keys.

## *Cryptography*

Cryptography is the practice of secure communication, which involves the use of mathematical techniques to encode and decode messages to protect their confidentiality, integrity, and authenticity. It is an essential component of many security systems, including those used on the Web.

In the context of Web 3.0 and blockchain, cryptography is used to secure the data within a blockchain and ensure that it cannot be altered or deleted without being detected. This is accomplished through the use of cryptographic hash functions, which are mathematical algorithms that take an input of any size and produce a fixed-size output, known as a hash.

One of the key uses of cryptographic hash functions in blockchain is to create a unique code, called a hash, for each block in the chain. The hash of a block is created using the data within the block and the hash of the previous block, which ensures that any changes to the data in a block will result in a different hash value. This makes it virtually impossible to alter the data within a block without being detected.

Cryptography is also used in blockchain to secure transactions within a block. When a transaction is added to a block, it is typically encoded using a public key encryption algorithm, which involves the use of a pair of keys: a public key, which is used to encrypt the data, and a private key, which is used to decrypt it. This ensures that only the intended recipient can read the transaction, while anyone else who intercepts it will not be able to decode it.

In addition to hash functions and encryption algorithms, blockchain may also use other cryptographic techniques, such as digital signatures, to ensure the authenticity of transactions and prevent tampering.

Overall, the use of cryptography in blockchain is essential for ensuring the security and integrity of the data within them. It allows blockchain to be used as a secure and transparent platform for recording and verifying transactions and other types of data, which makes them a valuable tool for Web 3.0 and many other applications.

## Solidity
Solidity is a high-level, object-oriented language that may be used to construct smart contracts. Programs known as smart contracts control how accounts behave in the Ethereum state. The curly bracket language Solidity is intended to work with the Ethereum Virtual Machine (EVM) [13]. It is influenced by JavaScript, Python, and C++. In the section on linguistic influences, you may read more information about the languages that Solidity was influenced by. In addition to supporting inheritance, libraries, and sophisticated user-defined types, Solidity is statically typed. You may design contracts using Solidity for applications like voting, crowdsourcing, blind bidding, and multi-signature wallets. Use Solidity's most recent public release for installing contracts. Only the most recent version gets security updates, barring rare circumstances.

## IPFS
A peer-to-peer hypermedia protocol designed to preserve and grow humanity's knowledge by making the web upgradeable, resilient, and more open.

A decentralized storage system is the Interplanetary File System (IPFS). a distributed file system protocol and peer-to-peer (p2p) network for storing, accessing, and sharing data. It is built on ContentBased Identity (CID), also known as Content-Based Addressing, which was designed to save data more quickly than the conventional Location-Based Addressing method.

## MetaMask
MetaMask is a browser extension that allows users to interact with the Ethereum blockchain. It serves as a wallet for storing, sending, and receiving Ethereum and other Ethereum-based tokens, and it allows users to interact with decentralized applications (dApps) on the Ethereum network.

## Alchemy
Alchemy is a blockchain infrastructure platform that provides developers with tools and services for building and scaling decentralized applications (dApps). It is designed to make it easier for developers to build and deploy dApps, and it provides a range of features such as secure key management, scalable data storage, and real-time analytics.

## React

React is a JavaScript library for building user interfaces. It was developed by Facebook and is often used for building single-page applications and mobile applications. It allows developers to create reusable UI components, which can be combined to build complex user interfaces. It uses a virtual DOM (Document Object Model) to optimize the rendering of components, so that only the parts of the UI that have changed are updated, rather than the entire UI. This can make applications built with React more efficient and performant.

## Node

Node.js is an open-source, cross-platform JavaScript runtime environment that executes JavaScript code outside of a web browser. It allows developers to run JavaScript on the server-side to create server-side applications with JavaScript.

Node.js is built on top of the V8 JavaScript engine, which was developed by Google for use in the Chrome web browser. It uses an event-driven, non-blocking I/O model, which makes it lightweight and efficient for building scalable network applications.

## Ether

Ether.js is a JavaScript library for interacting with the Ethereum blockchain. It provides a simple, easy-to-use interface for developers to build Ethereum applications, and it is designed to make it easier to work with the Ethereum blockchain and Ethereum-based smart contracts.

Ether.js provides a number of features that make it useful for developers working with the Ethereum blockchain. Some of these features include:

- Support for Ethereum JSON-RPC API: Ether.js provides support for the Ethereum JSON-RPC API, which allows developers to send transactions and interact with smart contracts on the Ethereum blockchain.
- Support for smart contract deployment and interaction: Ether.js makes it easy for developers to deploy and interact with smart contracts on the Ethereum blockchain.
- Support for ERC20 and ERC721 tokens: Ether.js provides support for the ERC20 and ERC721 token standards, which are widely used for representing digital assets on the Ethereum blockchain.
- Overall, Ether.js is a useful tool for developers who want to build applications on the Ethereum blockchain, as it provides an easy-to-

use interface for interacting with the Ethereum blockchain and smart contracts.

## Results and Discussion

This methodology enables users to store his/her sensitive information on the blockchain, with the help of an easy-to-use website. Making it secure and easily accessible all over the internet.

As the result of the above research and finding an attempt has been made to develop an application capable of storing identity information on IPFS using WEB3.storage. Furthermore, the unique hash obtained from the IPFS is then stored in a database. At this point of time the user can access his/her data through this application. When someone demands the data by meeting the conditions for the blockchain contract, the contract executes itself and encrypts the CID with his public key and makes a transaction in the blockchain registry. Hence, the user now has access to the required data after decrypting it with his/her private key. This in turn increases the security to a great extent [14].

Below (Figure 5) are some proof of work for the described application.

In the welcome page (Figure 5), user can login and store his/her information on IPFS, as well as can view his/her stored data.

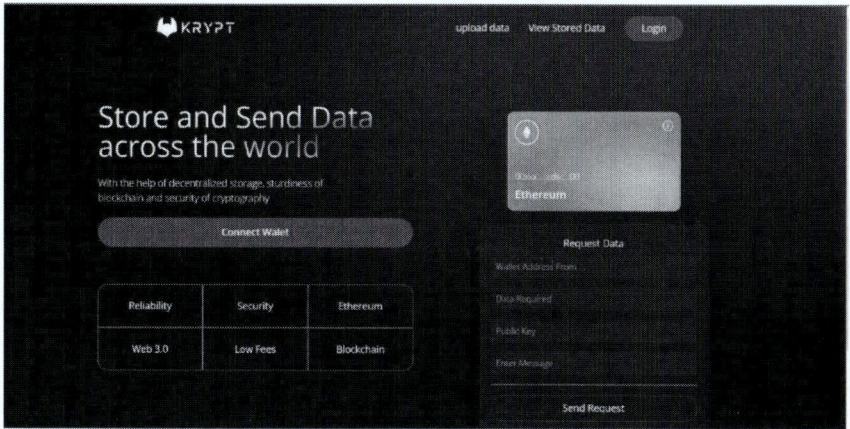

**Figure 5.** Showing the Welcome Page for the Application.

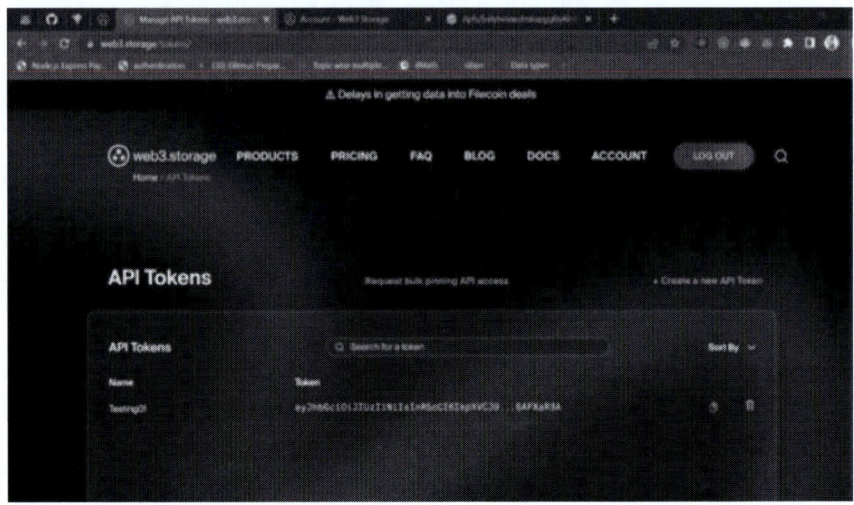

**Figure 6.** The User After Logging in Creates API Token Required for Storing the Data on IPFS.

The user creates API token (see Figure 6) required for storing the data on IPFS. In Figure 7, code for pushing data is shown. While Figure 8, depicts the demo of a file being stored on IPFS.

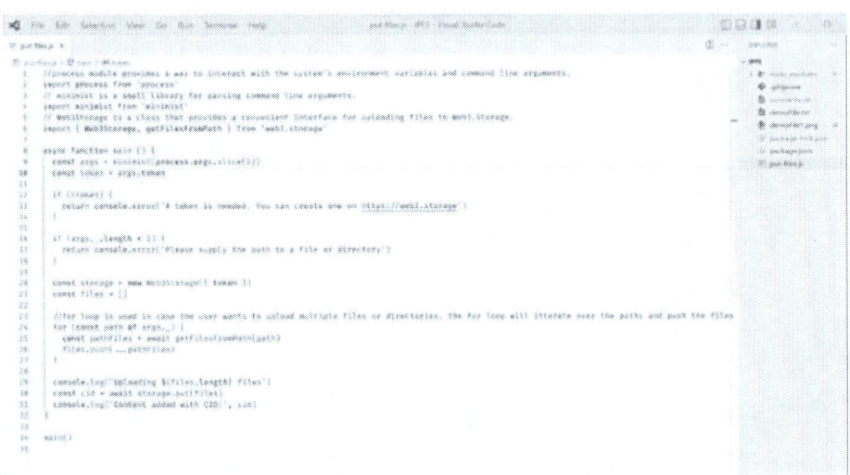

**Figure 7.** Code For Pushing Data on the IPFS Using WEB3.Storage API.

Enhancing Data Storage Security Using Web3 and Cryptography 81

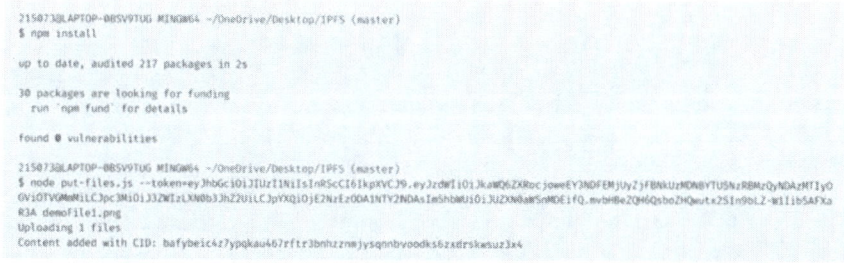

**Figure 8.** Demo of a File Being Stored on IPFS.

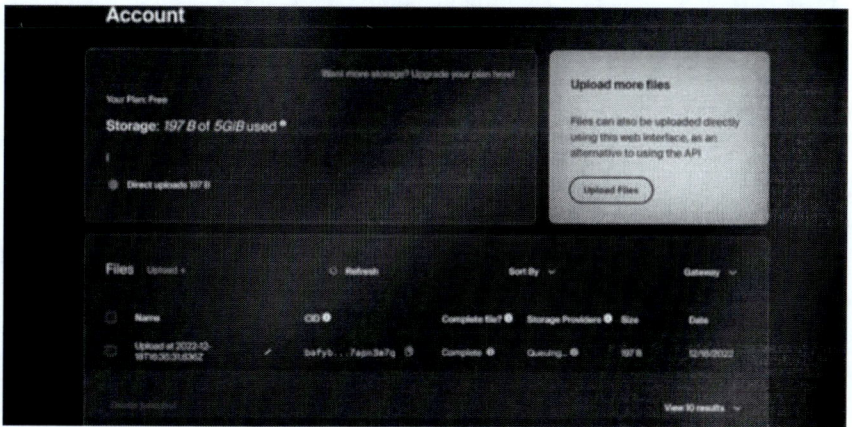

**Figure 9.** The User can Check His/her Data on the Web3.Storage Site.

The above Figure 9 depicts how a user can check the stored data on the Web3 site as well. Figure 10 depicts how a user can track data from the application concerned by clicking on a link.

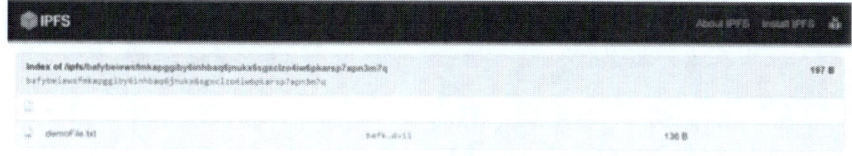

**Figure 10.** The User can also Track His/her Data from the Concerned Application by Clicking on a Link.

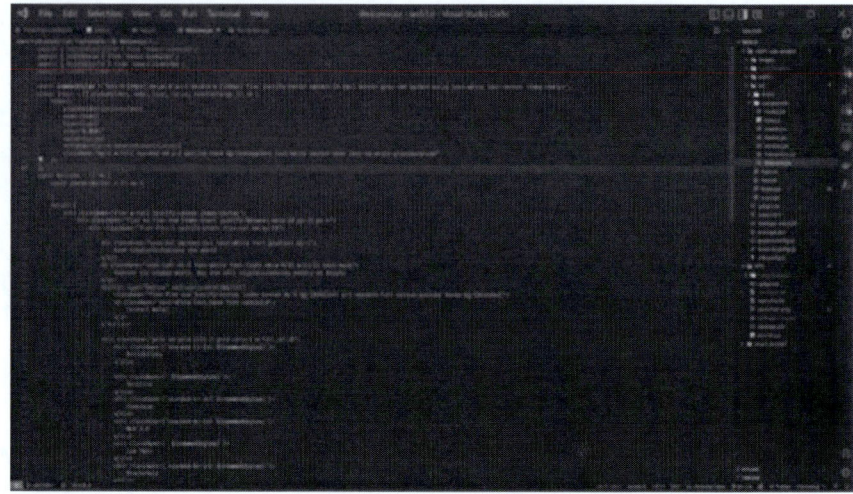

**Figure 11.** Code for the Welcome Page of the Application.

Figure 11 shows the code for the welcome page of the application and Figure 12 shows the page for uploading CID number.

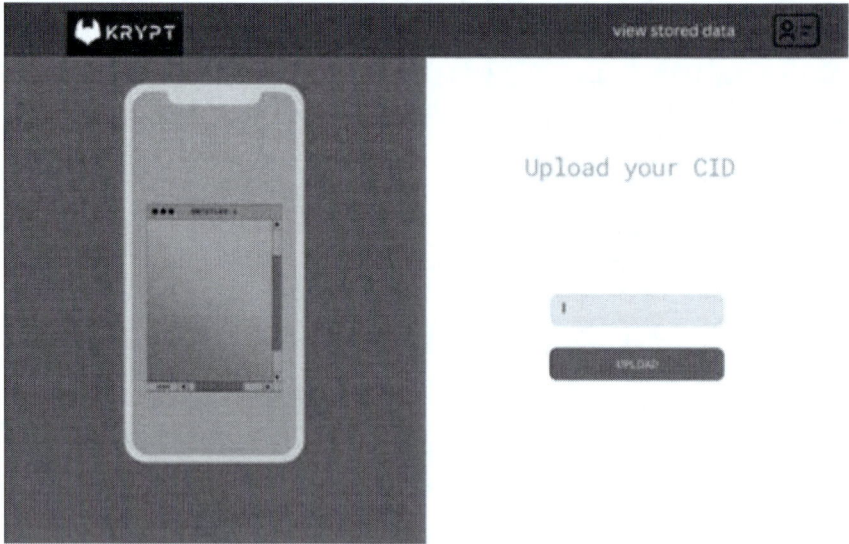

**Figure 12.** Page for Uploading CID Number.

Enhancing Data Storage Security Using Web3 and Cryptography 83

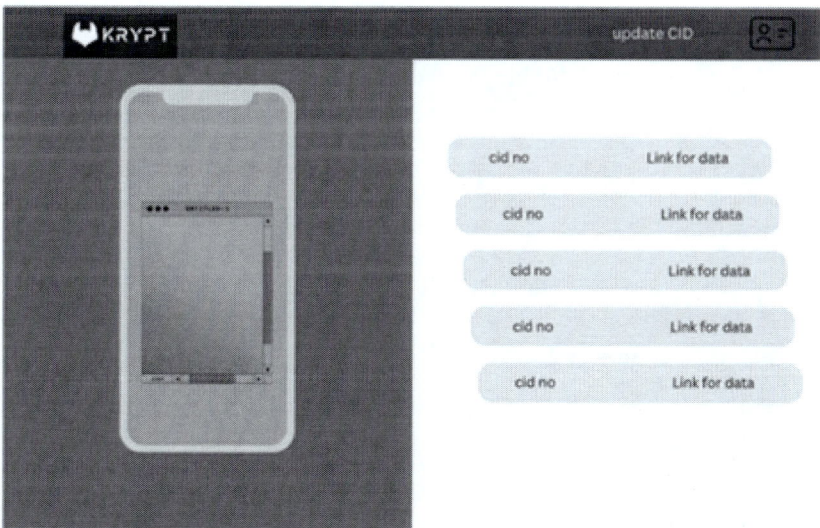

**Figure 13.** Page Showing All the Data with Access to Particular Login.

Figure 13 in this chapter depicts the page showing all the data with access to particular login and Figure 14 depicts the page for requesting data access from concerned walled.

**Figure 14.** Page for Requesting Data Access from Concerned Walled.

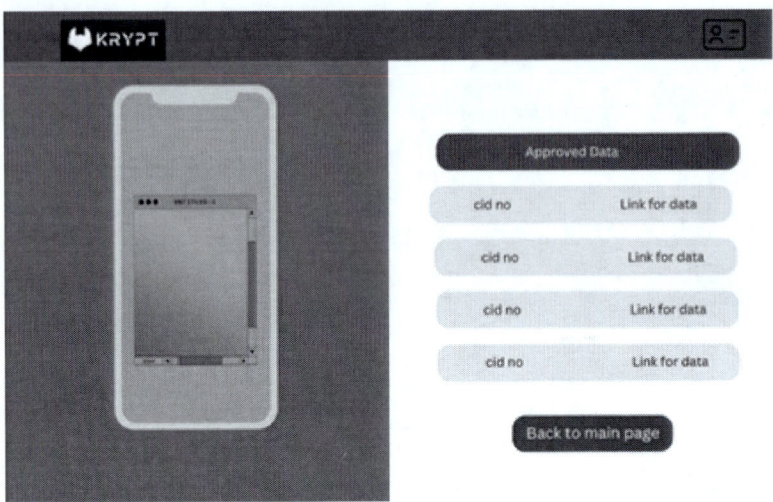

**Figure 15.** Page for Checking All the Approved Data in Case if the Contract Executes Successfully.

Figure 15 shows the page for checking all the approved data in case if the contract executes successfully whereas Figure 16 depicts the page for asking the user to get back to the main page in case there is some error in contract execution.

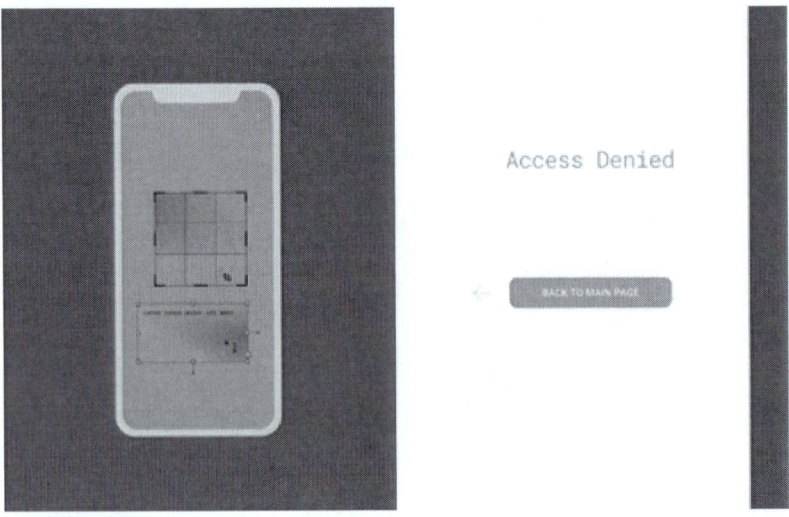

**Figure 16.** Page for Asking the User to Get Back to the Main Page in Case There is Some Error in Contract Execution.

## Future Scope

At this point, IPFS feels to be one of the best options for decentralized storage. As the future as technology advances, there will be more and more solutions available in the market which can be used to enhance the security of the application. Furthermore, an interface can also be designed for integrating the IPFS portal which automatically stores the CID number in the application's database. And during the transaction it aids the user.

## Conclusion

Blockchain technology and cryptography together can be used to enhance the security and privacy of identity storage. Here are a few ways in which this can be done:

- Storing identity data on a blockchain: By storing identity data on a blockchain, it can be made more secure and immutable. A blockchain is a decentralized, distributed database that stores data in blocks that are linked and secured using cryptographic techniques. This means that data stored on a blockchain is difficult to alter or delete, making it more secure than traditional databases.
- Using cryptographic techniques to secure identity data: Cryptography can be used to secure identity data in various ways. For example, identity data can be encrypted using a strong encryption algorithm to protect it from unauthorized access. In addition, cryptographic techniques such as digital signatures can be used to verify the authenticity of identity data.
- Using decentralized identity systems: Decentralized identity systems use blockchain technology to enable individuals to control their own identity data. This means that individuals can choose which identity data they share and with whom, increasing their privacy and control over their personal information.

Overall, using blockchain technology and cryptography can help to enhance the security and privacy of identity storage, making it more difficult for identity data to be accessed or altered without permission.

Furthermore, A trust framework is necessary for the decentralized personality of the board. It enables users to design and manage their own computerized personalities without depending on a certain

By providing accessible and unchangeable data repositories, blockchain has aided in the development of Web3. Figure 3 shows the architecture of blockchain, where the items in the red dotted area were not included in the initial Bitcoin concept. Because users wouldn't be able to confirm the system's state without a similar structure, a decentralized system without one would not operate as intended. In such a case, users of the system would, at best, lack faith that the system carries out their requested tasks successfully. Uncertainty obviously makes a system useless. Blockchain technology has made several strides recently, most of which are centered on analyzing and enhancing the original blockchain, bitcoin.

# References

[1] Ritterband, L. M., Gonder-Frederick, L. A., Cox, D. J., Clifton, A. D., West, R. W., and Borowitz, S. M. (2003). *Internet interventions: In review, in use, and into the future. Professional Psychology: Research and Practice*, 34(5), 527–534. doi:10.1037/0735-7028.34.5.527.

[2] Cerf, V. G. (2004). "On the evolution of Internet technologies," in *Proceedings of the IEEE*, vol. 92, no. 9, pp. 1360-1370, Aug., doi: 10.1109/JPROC.2004.832974.

[3] Kim, Y. C., Jung, J. Y., Cohen, E. L., and Ball-Rokeach, S. J. (2004). Internet connectedness before and after September 11 2001. New Media & Society, 6(5), 611–631. https://doi.org/10.1177/146144804047083.

[4] XRDS: Crossroads, The ACM Magazine for Students Volume 13 Issue 1 September 2006 pp. 3 https://doi.org/10.1145/1217666.1217669.

[5] Hendler, J. (2009). "Web 3.0 Emerging," in *Computer*, vol. 42, no. 1, pp. 111-113, Jan., doi: 0.1109/MC.2009.30.

[6] Rudman, R., and Bruwer, R. (2016). "Defining Web 3.0: opportunities and challenges", *The Electronic Library*, Vol. 34 No. 1, pp. 132-154. https://doi.org/10.1108/EL-08-2014-0140.

[7] Shukla, S., Gupta, I., and Naresh, K. (2022). "Addressing Security Issues and Future Prospects of Web 3.0," *2022 2nd Asian Conference on Innovation in Technology (ASIANCON)*, pp. 1-7, doi: 10.1109/ASIANCON55314.2022.9908800.

[8] Jing, Y., Li, J., Wang, Y., and Li, H. (2021). "The Introduction of Digital Identity Evolution and the Industry of Decentralized Identity," *2021 3rd International Academic Exchange Conference on Science and Technology Innovation (IAECST)*, pp. 504-508, doi: 10.1109/IAECST54258.2021.9695553.

[9] Weitzner, D. J. (2007). "Whose Name Is It, Anyway? Decentralized Identity Systems on the Web," in *IEEE Internet Computing*, vol. 11, no. 4, pp. 72-76, July-Aug., doi: 10.1109/MIC.2007.95.

[10] Data Storage in the Decentralized World: Blockchain and Derivatives, In Gulsecen S., Sharma S., Akadal E.(Eds.), Istanbul, Istanbul University Press (2020), https://doi.org/10.48550/arXiv.2012.10253.

[11] Shah, M., Shaikh, M., Mishra, V., and Tuscano, G. (2020). "Decentralized Cloud Storage Using Blockchain," *2020 4th International Conference on Trends in Electronics and Informatics (ICOEI)*, (48184), pp. 384389, doi: 10.1109/ICOEI48184.2020.9143004.

[12] Jianjun, S., Ming, L., and Jingang, M. (2020). "Research and application of data sharing platform integrating Ethereum and IPFs Technology," *2020 19th International Symposium on Distributed Computing and Applications for Business Engineering and Science (DCABES)*, pp. 279-282, doi: 10.1109/DCABES50732.2020.00079.

[13] Liang, W., Fan, Y., Li, K. C., Zhang, D., and Gaudiot, J. L. (2020). "Secure Data Storage and Recovery in Industrial Blockchain Network Environments," in *IEEE Transactions on Industrial Informatics*, vol. 16, no. 10, pp. 6543-6552, Oct., doi: 10.1109/TII.2020.2966069.

[14] Narayan, S., Mateen, A., Jeong, J. W., and Nam, S. Y. (2022). "Blockchain and IPFS-based Data Storage for VANET," *2022 13th International Conference on Information and Communication Technology Convergence (ICTC)*, pp. 1650-1653, doi: 10.1109/ICTC55196.2022.9952736.

## Chapter 6

# Securing Electronic Healthcare Records Using Blockchain: Is It a Viable Solution

## Pooja Saigal[*]
Vivekananda School of Professional Studies, Technical Campus, Delhi, India

### Abstract

Electronic Healthcare Records (EHRs) are essential sources of highly private information that must routinely be exchanged across peers in the healthcare industry, to enable comprehensive data analysis and deliver individualised healthcare. The sharing of EHRs is hampered by the healthcare companies' cyber infrastructure boundaries and potential privacy leaks. Blockchain, a decentralised public ledger known for its accountability, trust, and decentralisation, can aid in the construction of a network for secure medical data exchange. There is a rare chance to create a safe and reliable blockchain-based EHR data management and sharing system. This study examines the most cutting-edge approaches for sharing medical data securely and privately during the last few years, with a particular emphasis on blockchain-based methods. This chapter presents the views on healthcare data management based on blockchain technology and prospective study areas for exchanging medical data via blockchain.

**Keywords:** electronic healthcare records, security, blockchain approaches, encryption, access control in blockchain

---

[*] Corresponding Author's Email: pooja.saigal@vips.edu.

In: Blockchain and EHR
Editors: Kavita Saini, Amar Kumar and J. N. Singh
ISBN: 979-8-89113-380-8
© 2024 Nova Science Publishers, Inc.

## Introduction

Data is created, shared, stored, and retrieved often in the data-intensive industry of healthcare. When a patient has certain tests (such as computerised tomography or computerized axial tomography scans), for instance, data is generated, and it must be shared with the radiographer and subsequently a doctor. The outcomes of the visit will then be kept on file at the hospital, where a doctor in another hospital within the network may need to access them in the future. Paper-based data is difficult to convert in digital form due to costly data input mistakes, expensive to archive, and not always readily accessible. These issues could result in incomplete information being used to make medical decisions. This would further create the need for additional testing because of missing data or data being stored in a different hospital in a different state or country (at the expense of raising costs and creating inconvenience for the patients), etc. The importance of protecting the security, privacy, and integrity of healthcare data stems from the nature of the sector. This emphasises the necessity of an efficient and reliable data management system. Technology may significantly improve patient care (e.g., by utilising data analytics to make knowledgeable medical decisions) and perhaps lower costs by more effectively allocating resources (e.g., employees, equipment, etc.).

Electronic Medical Records (EMRs) typically include medical and clinical information specific to a particular patient that has been saved by the accountable healthcare provider. This makes it easier to retrieve and analyze medical data. Early Health Information Systems (HIS) [1] are created with the capacity to create new EMR instances, store them, and query and retrieve stored EMRs of interest in order to better support the administration of EMRs. HIS may involve rather straightforward solutions, which are conceptually equivalent to a graphical user interface or a web service. These often have a database at the back end and are implemented either centralizedly or decentralizedly. It became clear that several stand-alone EMR solutions needed to be made interoperable because patient mobility (both within and outside of a given country) is becoming more and more common in today's society. This will enable the sharing of healthcare data among various providers, even across international borders, as necessary. For instance, the demand for real-time healthcare data sharing between various providers and between nations becomes more obvious in medical tourism hotspots like Singapore [2].

EMRs must codify their data structure and HIS architecture in order to enable data exchange or even patient data portability. Electronic Health

Records (EHRs), for instance, are made to make it possible for a patient's medical history to travel with them or be made accessible to a variety of healthcare providers (for instance, from a rural hospital to a hospital in the nation's capital before the patient seeks treatment at another hospital in another nation) [3]. Compared to EMRs, EHRs feature a richer data structure. Various national and international initiatives, including the Fascicolo Sanitario Elettronico (FSE) project in Italy, the epSOS project in Europe, and a project to standardise the sharing of EHRs [4-5], demonstrate the efforts made to develop HIS and infrastructures that can scale and support future needs.

The widespread use of smart technologies, such as wearable technology and Android and iOS devices, has recently caused a paradigm shift in the healthcare sector. Such devices can be used by patients to monitor their well-being or implanted by healthcare professionals to inform and assist patient monitoring and medical treatment. For instance, there are numerous mobile applications in the healthcare-related areas of health, fitness, weight loss, and others. These apps primarily serve as tracking tools, recording user workouts and exercises, tracking calories consumed and other statistics (such the number of steps done), and so forth. For more complex medical duties, there are additional devices with embedded sensors, such as bracelets that detect heartbeat during exercise or gadgets for self-testing glucose. Leu and friends developed a smartphone-based wireless body sensor network to gather user physiological data utilising body sensors integrated into a smart shirt [6]. The information, such as the user's vital signs, can be continually captured and transmitted in real-time to a smart device before being forwarded to a remote healthcare cloud for additional analysis. Another example is Ambient Assisted Living, a type of healthcare solution created to implement cutting-edge telehealth and telemedicine services and offer remote personal health monitoring [7].

These advancements have opened the way for Personal Health Records (PHR), where patients are more actively involved in data collecting, condition monitoring, etc. utilising their smartphones or wearable technology [8]. However, there are a number of difficulties with PHRs. Can this information be trusted, which is gathered by the patients themselves? Should the relevant healthcare professionals certify the information gathered by the patients, and if yes, how? Who should be held accountable for judgements made based on data sent by the patient's device that were later shown to be defective or inaccurate (for example, because of a defective sensor) and resulted in wrong or delayed diagnosis?

Despite these difficulties and potentially complex legal issues, having an HIS based on an ecosystem of solutions that can exchange data in real-time and offer the abstraction of a single health data storage for any given patient will be advantageous to all users, including patients, healthcare providers, and governments.

## Need for Security and Privacy

Sensitive information is found in healthcare data, which could be appealing to cybercriminals. For instance, cybercriminals looking to profit financially from the theft of such data might sell the data to a third-party provider, who might then analyse the data to find people who might not be eligible for insurance due to their medical history or genetic disease. Some organisations or industries would be interested in such data. Data from EMRs, particularly Protected Health Information (PHI), is at even higher risk. Recent research [9] revealed an increase in the annual number of medical records that were made public. There are now more than one healthcare data breaches every day.

Most hospitals and healthcare organisations have improved security measures to prevent privacy leaking. They opt to construct their healthcare systems in a closed domain with a protective perimeter, such as a private network outfitted with firewalls and intrusion detection systems. A medical organization's current IT infrastructure deployments are often built on private cloud designs, which have restrictions on scalability and data exchange. A private cloud is a cloud computing model where information technology services are made available over a private network for the exclusive use of a single company. As a result, there are now numerous healthcare facilities with scattered medical data silos, making it difficult to conduct joint medical research and healthcare. Private cloud-based approaches require a significant investment in computing and storage devices to build highly scalable private clouds, and because the volume of clinical data is changing so quickly that it is difficult to predict the required cloud capacity in the future. This makes it difficult for collaborators who live outside of the domain perimeter to access data. Due to these restrictions, big data analytics cannot facilitate the increased sharing of medical data.

On the other side, the age of big data and cloud computing demands that medical data be shared with several users and institutions to enable analysis, allowing for the provision of better healthcare services and innovative treatment plans [10]. Because of the interplay and complexity between the systems and components, it is important to ensure the security of the EMR/EHR/PHR ecosystem and the underlying systems and components that make up the ecosystem. In addition, the confidentiality and integrity of healthcare data must be safeguarded against illegal access attempts from both inside and outside the network or ecosystem (e.g., employee at the healthcare facility, or those working for the cloud service provider). Organizations may face penalties or be charged with crimes in connection with attacks (such as data leaks or modifications), for example under the Health Insurance Portability and Accountability Act (HIPAA) [11] in the United States or the General Data Protection Regulation (GDPR) [12] in Europe.

The following issues are the main barriers to the safe and private sharing of clinical data:

- *Privacy and Security:* Medical data should be protected both while it is in use and while it is stored, with the standard security objectives of data confidentiality, integrity, and availability being met. Currently, the security of data in transit can be ensured using the Transport Layer Security (TLS) protocol. Cryptography primitives including data encryption, digital signatures, and access control techniques can guarantee safe access in a single domain for data that is at rest. However, it is still difficult to implement cross-domain access control and secure sharing of medical data on a state- or even national-scale. Although it has some similarities to security, privacy ensures that personal information is gathered, handled, and protected in accordance with the law. For instance, the privacy compliance regulations mandate that security and privacy standards be consistently followed for all actions involving electronic Protected Health Information (ePHI), including data storage, transfer, and provision.The challenge, in general, is that healthcare information's security and privacy must be safeguarded not only from external attackers but also against unauthorised access from within the network or system. Therefore, new approaches, designs, or computer paradigms may be required to address security and privacy issues in the domain of sharing medical data [13].
- *Increasing Amount of Data:* Medical data are vast in size and are growing in volume at a pace of 20–40% annually. Examples include X-ray images, CT scans, genetic data etc. An average US healthcare practitioner had to manage 665 gigabytes of patient data in 2015, of which 80% were unstructured medical pictures. It was predicted that

25,000 petabytes of big data would be used in healthcare by 2020 [13]. The difficulties involve not only storing such a large volume of data with the current IT infrastructure, but also safeguarding its integrity and confidentiality while preserving high availability among clinicians, medical researchers, and partners.

- *Cross-Institutional Data Sharing Barriers:* In order to fend off outside attacks and threats, the majority of current healthcare systems are constructed on an enclosed domain with a network security perimeter. This is a significant barrier to inter-institutional data sharing. Data access from outside the domain is restricted by its perimeter and cyberinfrastructure, and each autonomous domain often has its own data management policy, making it challenging to ensure compatibility between any two domains. Lack of data interoperability on medical information is a direct result of this network defence perimeter, which further creates a barrier for medical analytics that need a lot of clinical data. Additionally, it becomes a hassle for patients looking for better treatment plans when their medical records are dispersed throughout several facilities. Any bounded hospital ecosystem constructed on a private network is referred to as a healthcare domain, and any external access to internal databases and devices must be made through authenticated connections, like Virtual Private Networks (VPNs). It is a frequently used architecture for the administration of healthcare data today. Consequently, a more comprehensive and integrated healthcare infrastructure is required to enable secure data sharing and cooperation among different healthcare domains, as well as collaborative healthcare service and research.

## Blockchain for Securing Electronic Healthcare Records

Recently, there has been interest in using blockchain for secure healthcare data management. Blockchain is a technology made well-known by the success of Bitcoin [14]. In general, blockchain is a technology that can create an open, distributed online database made up of a list of data structures (sometimes referred to as blocks) that are connected to one another (i.e., a block points to the following one, hence the name blockchain). These blocks are not centrally kept; rather, they are dispersed among several infrastructure nodes. Each block includes a timestamp for when it was created, the preceding block's hash, transaction data, and in this case, information about a patient's medical history and their healthcare provider.

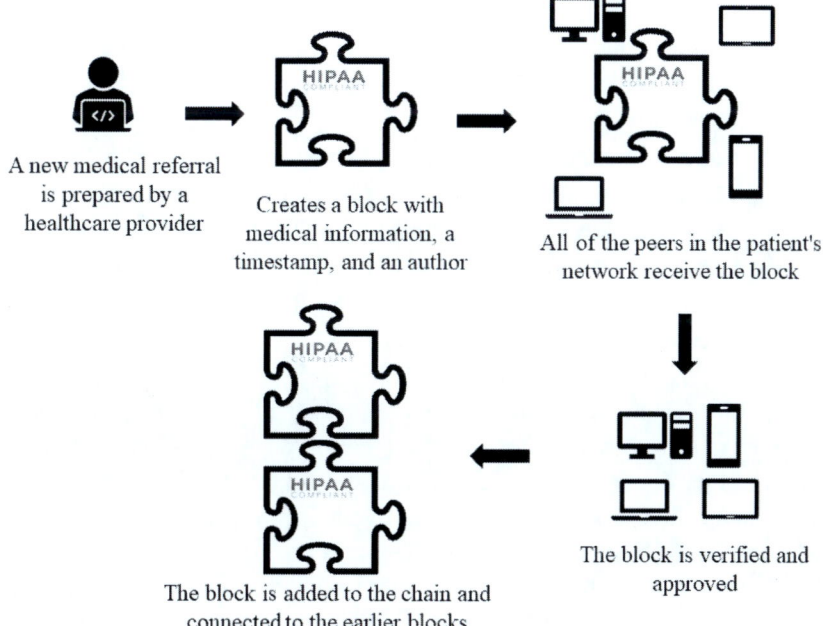

**Figure 1.** Hypothetical Blockchain Ecosystem.

A hypothetical blockchain-based EMR/EHR/PHR ecosystem is shown in Figure 1. Specifically, a new block is instantiated and disseminated to all peers in the patient network whenever new healthcare data is created for a specific patient (for example, from a consultation or medical procedure such as a surgery). The system will add the new block to the chain once it has received the majority of peer approval. This enables the healthcare professionals to efficiently, permanently, and verifiably obtain a comprehensive understanding of the patient's medical history. If no consensus is achieved, the chain forks, designating the block as an orphan and separating it from the main chain [15]. The data in any individual block cannot be changed once it has been entered into the chain, without also changing all blocks that come after it. In other words, it is simple to spot modifications. Prior to being included in the block, healthcare data must be safeguarded because the block's content is publicly available (e.g., obfuscated and perhaps, encrypted).

Blockchain technology is conceptually secure by design, offering the capacity to create decentralised consensus and consistency as well as resistance to malicious and/or accidental attacks [15]. The following are some of the main advantages of using a blockchain:

- In order to avoid a performance hiccup and a single point of failure, it is possible to reach agreements without the assistance of a trusted third party
- Patients retain control over their data
- Medical history data stored on a blockchain is complete, consistent, up to date, accurate, and simple to distribute
- Changes to the blockchain are visible to all in the patient network
- All data insertions are immutable. Furthermore, any unlawful alterations are easily detectable.

A blockchain-based method has limits that need to be carefully considered, as with any security solution. For instance, blockchain technology can be rather disruptive and necessitates an ecosystem-wide radical rethink and major investment (e.g., replacement of prevailing systems and restructuring of business processes). To put it another way, before making a decision, healthcare providers, especially those that are publicly financed, must conduct a cost-benefit analysis to comprehend the return on investment and any potential ramifications (e.g., legal and financial). The same record, for instance, might be spread across several network nodes in various nations with various privacy and data protection laws (e.g., EU and US).

## Challenges with Blockchain Technology

Blockchain's distributed storage, access and data integrity present benefits for managing healthcare data, but they also present problems that require more research [16].

- *Deletion of records:* Since blockchain technology has excellent data integrity, any data that has been saved there cannot be changed or destroyed. The right to request the deletion of personal data has been strengthened by Article 17 of the EU's General Data Protection Regulation. If the record pertains to healthcare, however, privacy

laws would protect it and many of them would not permit personal data to be kept indefinitely. The right-to-erasure is one of the tenets of the Organization for Economic Cooperation and Development privacy guideline, upon which many data protection laws are founded. Anyone who intends to use blockchain to store healthcare data must adhere to this legal requirement to delete personal data as necessary, given how sensitive this data is.
- Whether blockchain technology is appropriate for storing healthcare data is a further practical concern. Blockchain was initially intended to store transaction data, which is often linear and tiny in size. To put it another way, the only thing that matters is if the present transaction can be linked to the initial "deal." However, healthcare data might be big and relational, requiring searches, such as imaging and treatment plans. It's not yet apparent how well blockchain storage will work with both criteria [16].
- *Regulatory Compliance:* Business associates are subject to the security and privacy obligations of HIPAA and the HITECH Act [17]. These recommendations state that if patient data is accessed, saved, or transferred, all appropriate safeguards must be in place. HIPAA security standards non-compliance could result in hefty fines and, in some situations, the loss of medical licences. In addition to the fundamental needs for traditional information security, such as confidentiality, integrity, and authentication, there are now new requirements for access control with identity tracking and emergency access, as well as activity auditing. HIPAA rule essentially covers every area of security covering technical safeguard standards and implementation requirements [17], as listed below:
  a) Access control involves identifying and tracking user identities, a process for obtaining documents in an emergency, and an encryption-decryption mechanism for health records.
  b) Audit control involves documenting and examining activity that involves EHR.
  c) Integrity involves a mechanism to prevent EHR from being changed without authorization.
  d) Authentication: Steps taken to ensure the identity of any entity requesting access to EHR.
  e) Transmission Security: Security mechanisms to ensure that records sent electronically are not unlawfully altered without

detection until disposal and a mechanism to encrypt EHR when considered necessary.

## Protocols for Blockchain

Many researchers are currently thinking about using blockchain to secure medical data exchange and administration, in light of the adoption of blockchain technology becoming a widely accepted trend in distributed computing. These schemes fall into two categories: permissioned and permissionless blockchain-based approaches.

### Permissionless Blockchain Approaches

- Blockchain technology was suggested by Zyskind and fellow researchers provided a means of enabling safe and private data sharing between mobile users and service providers. Their architecture suggests two different sorts of transactions, namely transaction $T_{data}$ and transaction $T_{access}$, which are utilised for access control and data storage and retrieval respectively.
- A working prototype version of MedRec [18], a decentralised EHR management system built on blockchain technology, is available. Three different types of Ethereum smart contracts have been created by MedRec to link patient medical records from different healthcare organisations so that, after successful verification, third parties can access the information. Registerar contracts specifically map node identification strings to their Ethereum addresses. The ownership of a patient's clinical data are specified in a patient-provider relationship (PPR) contract, together with access rights and query strings specifying data positions. A list of PPR references is kept in a summary contract to show the engagements with other patient nodes or hospital nodes.
- A blockchain-based architecture with a purpose centric access control policy was described by Yue and fellow researchers [19] as a healthcare data gateway that enables patients to own, control, and share their medical information without compromising privacy. However, their plan doesn't specify how a service is kept from

knowing the substance of the data when a computation is conducted on the raw medical data.
- Yang and Yang [20] suggested employing attribute-based authentication and signcryption to allow for the secure sharing of medical data. A symmetric key that has been further encrypted with an attribute key set is used to encrypt EHRs. A private key is used to sign the concatenation of the two ciphertexts (the encrypted key and the encrypted EHRs). To access data, a user must verify the signature, decrypt the key, then decrypt the EHRs to obtain the plaintext EHRs.
- In order to handle keys that are needed to encrypt the health signals that were gathered from body sensor networks (BSN) and stored on a health blockchain, Zhao and fellow [21] advocated employing fuzzy vault technology. However, their work lacks specifics regarding how their health blockchain functions.
- In order to speed up medical research and enable quality enhancements, Modelchain [22] was created to adapt blockchain for privacy-preserving machine learning. To boost effectiveness and accuracy, the design uses a proof-of-information technique on top of the Proof-of-work (PoW) consensus protocol to decide the order of online machine learning.

These plans advocate using a permissionless or public blockchain to secure apps and the sharing of medical data (e.g., healthcare sensors, machine learning). A fixed amount of cryptocurrency must be paid for transaction inclusion and block mining on public blockchain, which is often cryptocurrency-driven (bitcoins in Bitcoin or ether in Ethereum). A public blockchain can be highly expensive to store data on. The cost of keeping millions of patients' thorough clinical records on a chain is too high. Instead, the blockchain can only be used to store a very small subset of vital metadata. In a public blockchain, data-related tasks like access requests, access policy verification, and message transfer can all be expensive since transactions describing them must be made.

## Permissioned Blockchain Approaches

- A blockchain-based strategy for inter-institutional sharing of health information was suggested by Peterson and other researchers [23]. To enable secure access to off-chain stored Fast Healthcare Interoperability Resources (FHIR), they created new transaction and block structures. They also created a new consensus algorithm that does not use the costly computational resources required by Bitcoin's PoW consensus. Before being added to the blockchain, a block would go through a distribution phase for transactions, a block verification request phase, a signed block return phase, and a new blockchain distribution phase. In their consensus process, a proof-of-interoperability idea was put forth to guarantee that transaction data adheres to FHIR's structural and semantic requirements. They also created a random miner election process that gives every node in the network an equal chance of eventually becoming a miner.

- Xia and co rerearchers introduced blockchain-based data sharing [24], a high-level blockchain-based framework that allows data consumers and owners to access medical information from a common repository, after successfully verifying their identities and keys.
- User membership authentication is accomplished in [25] via an identity-based authentication and key agreement system. However, they only allow invited and vetted users to securely share sensitive medical information.
- Fan and co researchers introduced MedBlock [26], a hybrid blockchain-based architecture that divides nodes into endorsers, orderers, and committers to safeguard electronic medical records (EMR).
- A modification of the Practical Byzantine Fault Tolerance (PBFT) [27] consensus process serves as its consensus protocol. However, the access control procedure used to grant outside researchers access to medical data was not made clear by the authors. Additionally, their suggestion that medical data be encrypted using asymmetric encryption techniques does not appear to be a viable choice when taking into account how well asymmetric encryption performs during encryption and decryption.
- According to Wang and other researchers [28] Parallel Healthcare System (PHS), artificial systems, computational experiments, and parallel executions are used to produce descriptive intelligence, predictive intelligence, and prescriptive intelligence in healthcare. A consortium blockchain that includes patients, hospitals, health bureaus and communities, and medical researchers is implemented in

its structure. To enable the sharing, reviewing, and auditing of medical records, smart contracts have been introduced.
- For the sharing of personal health data, Liang and fellow researchers [29] suggested a user-centric framework on a permissioned blockchain. Identity management and privacy protection are provided via the Hyperledger Fabric membership service and channel formation scheme. Utilizing a mobile app, they gather health information from wearable technology and sync it to the cloud for storage and sharing with healthcare professionals.
- A healthcare peer-to-peer EMR storage network called Patientory [30] uses smart contracts and the blockchain to facilitate HIPAA compliant health information exchange. Additionally, the authors put forth a software framework to handle token management, interoperability improvement, authentication, authorization, access control, and data encryption throughout system installation.
- For companies doing transactions in a permissioned blockchain, the ChainAnchor [31] solution offers anonymous identity verification. The system uses the Enhanced Privacy ID (EPID) zero-knowledge proof mechanism to validate the membership and anonymity of participants.

All these systems select a permissioned blockchain or a consortium to safeguard the storage of medical data. This contrasts with completely decentralised methods based on open-source blockchains like Bitcoin and Ethereum. Instead, access to the consortium blockchain requires specific authorization. This indicates that participants are chosen in advance, and that only those nodes who have been granted access can view data stored on the blockchain. In a situation like this, which is comparable to the sharing of medical data, only healthcare stakeholders—patients, healthcare professionals, and approved medical researchers—can be given access to the data depending on their permissions.

Permissioned blockchain is far from a perfect option for safe medical data sharing, despite its high throughput. The main drawback is the requirement for a central authority, which is typically made up of a collection of businesses with a common goal and will manage the blockchain network and supervise the entire system. As a result, the consortium blockchain disregards the data immutability of the public blockchain, which leaves room for a blockchain rollback by an attacker or a particular authority member.

## Blockchain: as a Viable Solution for Medical Data Sharing

These schemes discussed in the previous section give light on the blockchain use in medical data sharing and management, regardless of whether the chosen blockchain is permissioned or permissionless. Blockchain technology by itself, however, is not a magic bullet for all security and privacy issues in the exchange of medical data. We should be more conscious of the limitations of blockchain technology than its benefits so that we may integrate it with other strategies (such cryptographic primitives) to address the security issues with medical information management and make up for its drawbacks [31].

Patients, healthcare professionals, and outside medical researchers all share medical data securely. Medical data management should offer secure storage of unprocessed medical data (confidentiality, integrity), privacy-preserving data provision (data authenticity, user authentication, access control), auditability, traceability, and data interoperability, in accordance with HIPAA's privacy and security regulations. Additionally, when blockchain technology is used for healthcare data exchange, the following critical qualities may require more research [32].

1) Storage of medical data on or off-chain?
    a. Because blockchain was initially intended to record little trading transactions, its data capacity is typically constrained. For instance, the one megabyte maximum block size of Bitcoin makes it impossible to hold medical data like X-ray scans. There are yet more parts of the data cycle that require careful consideration. Because blockchain is a continuously expanding public ledger, data that is saved on the blockchain cannot be changed or removed. Since patients own their medical data, various rules, like the GDPR in Europe, have strengthened patients' rights to have their personal health information deleted. Since most data have a lifespan, it is not necessary to keep them indefinitely stored. Numerous laws protecting data privacy also enforce this [32].
    b. The blockchain itself is a safe and open public ledger that can ensure the accuracy of data stored there (transactions and blocks). Therefore, if we opt for onchain data storage, blockchain can be used to safeguard the storage of medical information. This naive strategy would, however, result in low throughput and performance because every peer node must locally download on-

chain transactions and blocks, which wastes a lot of bandwidth [33]. This explains why the majority of cutting-edge methods for exchanging medical data choose to store patient data off-chain while data query strings and hash values are stored on-chain for authenticity and integrity verification. Medical data can be secured, changed, and destroyed as needed in such an architecture.

2) Is data encryption required?
   a. It is clear from the research above that due to the present blockchains' limited block sizes and the bandwidth required for network consensus, on-chain storage of medical data is not a good option. Off-chain storage of medical data appears to be a workable substitute. We should be mindful of one truth, though, in this instance: blockchain can only ensure the security of data held on-chain.
   b. Therefore, to achieve its security and privacy objectives for such off-chain stored data, we still need to create data storage and access methods with suitable cryptographic primitives. Before continuing, it is important to determine whether off-chain stored medical data should be encrypted. A 2014 study [33] found that the medical sector accounts for over 50% of security breaches and that up to 90% of healthcare firms had either had their data exposed or stolen. It is clear that keeping medical records in plain text in a database will raise the danger of leaks, primarily for the reasons listed below:
      i. All medical information could be disclosed once a healthcare system is breached;
      ii. Despite the stringent access control policies used in a healthcare system, an inside IT technical staff member can still readily "access" the data, making data confidentiality difficult to ensure.

In this context, secure key storage and encryption of medical data are two essential measures to improve the security and privacy of medical data. When a healthcare system is breached, data encryption may be the last line of security since, absent the corresponding encryption key, an attacker cannot decipher the encrypted data.

3) Blockchain: Permissioned or Permissionless
   a. The primary difference between permissioned and permissionless blockchains is the consensus protocol that has

been implemented. This difference has a significant effect on throughput, block mining time, access regulations, and privacy.

b. The cryptocurrency that serves as the incentive for the underlying consensus protocol would be another obstacle to the adoption of permissionless blockchain for medical data sharing. Data access occurs frequently in the management of medical data [34]. This implies that a sizable sum of money (cryptocurrency) is required to maintain the network for managing healthcare data. To pay contributions, one approach is to create an altercoin within the system (miners) [35]. A contributor can receive better service in the system once they have a particular amount of Altercoin, which will raise their degree of trustworthiness.

## Conclusion

Sharing medical information while remaining compliant with security and privacy laws has always been a difficult problem. In this chaper, blockchain-based solutions are reviewed. It is found that the confidentiality, integrity, and authenticity of data in transit and at rest, as well as access and privacy control, are the most important factors to be acknowledged for privacy protection of medical information. The advantages of blockchain over conventional technologies are that it represents a new paradigm in computing. To share medical data, it is crucial to select the appropriate blockchain type (permissioned or permissionless). Additionally, there are still a few issues that warrant more research and development in blockchain-based medical data management. A lot of research needs to be done before using blockchain approaches that provide strengthened data security and make it easier to share medical records.

## References

[1] Steward, M., "Electronic Medical Records," *Journal of Legal Medicine*, vol. 26, no. 4, 2005, pp. 491–506.

[2] Hauxe, R., "Health Information Systems—Past, Present, Future," *Int'l Journal of Medical Informatics*, vol. 75, no. 3–4, 2006, pp. 268–281.

[3]  Häyrinen, Kristiina, Kaija Saranto, and Pirkko Nykänen. "Definition, structure, content, use and impacts of electronic health records : a review of the research literature." *International journal of medical informatics* 77, no. 5 (2008): 291-304.

[4]  Ciampi, Mario, Giuseppe De Pietro, Christian Esposito, Mario Sicuranza, and Paolo Donzelli. "A federated interoperability architecture for health information systems." *International Journal of Internet Protocol Technology* 7, no. 4 (2013): 189-202.

[5]  Han, S. H., Lee, M. H., Kim, S. G., Jeong, J. Y., Lee, B. N., Choi, M. S., Kim, I. K., Park, W. S., Ha, K., Cho, E. and Kim, Y., 2010. Implementation of medical information exchange system based on EHR standard. *Healthcare informatics research*, 16(4), pp.281-289.

[6]  You, Ilsun, Kim-Kwang Raymond Choo, and Chi-Lun Ho. "A smartphone-based wearable sensors for monitoring real-time physiological data." *Computers & Electrical Engineering* 65 (2018): 376-392.

[7]  Memon, Mukhtiar, Stefan Rahr Wagner, Christian Fischer Pedersen, Femina Hassan Aysha Beevi, and Finn Overgaard Hansen. "Ambient assisted living healthcare frameworks, platforms, standards, and quality attributes." *Sensors* 14, no. 3 (2014): 4312-4341.

[8]  Tang, Paul C., Joan S. Ash, David W. Bates, J. Marc Overhage, and Daniel Z. Sands. "Personal health records : definitions, benefits, and strategies for overcoming barriers to adoption." *Journal of the American Medical Informatics Association* 13, no. 2 (2006) : 121-126.

[9]  Healthcare Industry Ranks 8th for Cybersecurity but Poor DNS Health and Endpoint Security of Concern. [Online]. Available: https://www.hipaajournal.com/healthcare-data-breach-statistics/.

[10] Jin, Hao, Yan Luo, Peilong Li, and Jomol Mathew. "A review of secure and privacy-preserving medical data sharing." *IEEE Access* 7 (2019): 61656-61669.

[11] Summary of the HIPAA Security Rule. [Online]. Available: https://www.hhs.gov/hipaa/for-professionals/security/laws-regulations/.

[12] General Data Protection Regulation. [Online]. Available: https://eugdpr.org/the-regulation/.

[13] Raghupathi, W. and V. Raghupathi, "Big data analytics in healthcare: Promise and potential," *Health Inf. Sci. Syst.*, vol. 2, no. 1, p. 3, 2014.

[14] Tschorsch, F. and B. Scheuermann, "Bitcoin and Beyond: A Technical Survey on Decentralized Digital Currencies," *IEEE Communications Surveys & Tutorials*, vol. 18, no. 3, 2016, pp. 2084–2123.

[15] "Blockchain : A panacea for healthcare cloud-based data security and privacy?" *IEEE Cloud Comput.*, vol. 5, no. 1, pp. 31–37, Jan./Feb. 2018.

[16] McKinlay, J., D. Pithouse, J. McGonagle, and J. Sunders. *"Blockchain : background, challenges and legal issues, DLA Piper."* (2018). doi.org/https://www.dlapiper.com/en/uk/insights/publications/2017/06/blockchain background-challenges-legal-issues/.

[17] Zyskind, G., O. Nathan, and A. S. Pentland, "Decentralizing privacy: Using blockchain to protect personal data," in *Proc. IEEE Secur. Privacy Workshops* (SPW), May 2015, pp. 180–184.

[18] Azaria, A. Ekblaw, T. Vieira, and A. Lippman, "Medrec: Using blockchain for medical data access and permission management," in *Proc. 2nd Int. Conf. Open Big Data (OBD)*, Aug. 2016, pp. 25–30.

[19] Yue, X., H. Wang, D. Jin, M. Li, and W. Jiang, "Healthcare data gateways: Found healthcare intelligence on blockchain with novel privacy risk control," *J. Med. Syst.*, vol. 40, no. 10, pp. 218–225, 2016H.

[20] Yang and B. Yang, "A blockchain-based approach to the secure sharing of healthcare data," in *Proc. Norwegian Inf. Secur. Conf.*, 2017, pp. 1–12.

[21] Zhao, H., Y. Zhang, Y. Peng, and R. Xu, "Lightweight backup and efficient recovery scheme for health blockchain keys," in *Proc. IEEE 13th Int.Symp. Auton. Decentralized Syst. (ISADS)*, Mar. 2017, pp. 229–234.

[22] Kuo, T.-T., and L. Ohno-Machado. (2018). *"Modelchain: Decentralized privacy-preserving healthcare predictive modeling framework on private blockchain networks."* [Online]. Available: https://arxiv.org/abs/1802.01746.

[23] Peterson, K., R. Deeduvanu, P. Kanjamala, and K. Boles, "A blockchainbased approach to health information exchange networks," in *Proc. NIST Workshop Blockchain Healthcare*, vol. 1, 2016, pp. 1–10.

[24] Xia, Q., E. B. Sifah, A. Smahi, S. Amofa, and X. Zhang, "BBDS : Blockchain-based data sharing for electronic medical records in cloud environments," *Information*, vol. 8, no. 2, p. 44, 2017.

[25] Wu, L., Y. Zhang, Y. Xie, A. Alelaiw, and J. Shen, "An efficient and secure identity-based authentication and key agreement protocol with user anonymity for mobile devices," *Wireless Pers. Commun.*, vol. 94, no. 4, pp. 3371–3387, 2017.

[26] Saini, Kavita, Abhishek Roy, Pethuru Raj Chelliah, and Tanisha Patel. "Blockchain 2. O : A Smart Contract." In *2021 International Conference on Computational Performance Evaluation (ComPE)*, pp. 524-528. IEEE, 2021.

[27] Fan, K., S. Wang, Y. Ren, H. Li, and Y. Yang, "MedBlock: Efficient and secure medical data sharing via blockchain," *J. Med. Syst.*, vol. 42, no. 8, pp. 136–146, 2018.

[28] Castro, M. and B. Liskov, "Practical byzantine fault tolerance and proactive recovery," *ACM Trans. Comput. Syst.*, vol. 20, no. 4, pp. 398–461, 2002.

[29] Saini K, editor. *Blockchain and IoT Integration: Approaches and applications*. CRC Press; 2021 Oct 28.

[30] Wang, S., Wang, J., Wang, X., Qiu, T., Yuan, Y., Ouyang, L., Guo, Y. and Wang, F.Y., 2018. Blockchain-powered parallel healthcare systems based on the ACP approach. *IEEE Transactions on Computational Social Systems*, 5(4), pp.942-950.

[31] Liang, X., J. Zhao, S. Shetty, J. Liu, and D. Li, "Integrating blockchain for data sharing and collaboration in mobile healthcare applications," in *Proc. IEEE 28th Annu. Int. Symp. Pers., Indoor, Mobile Radio Commun. (PIMRC)*, Oct. 2017, pp. 1–5.

[32] Singh, A., G. Ajmera and J. N. Singh, "Data Analysis using ML on Geolocational Data," 2022 4th International Conference on Advances in Computing, Communication Control and Networking (ICAC3N), Greater Noida, India, 2022, pp. 6-10, doi: 10.1109/ICAC3N56670.2022.10074047.

[33] Gupta, V., J. N. Singh, S. I. Khan and A. Chabaque, "Blockchain-Based Electronic Voting System," 2022 4th International Conference on Advances in Computing, Communication Control and Networking (ICAC3N), Greater Noida, India, 2022, pp. 2049-2053, doi: 10.1109/ICAC3N56670.2022.10074384.

[34] McFarlane, C., M. Beer, J. Brown, and N. Prendergast, Patientory: A Healthcare Peer-to-Peer EMR Storage Network v1. Addison, TX, USA : Entrust, 2017.

[35] Hardjono, T., and A. Pentland. (2019). *"Verifiable anonymous identities and access control in permissioned blockchains."* [Online]. Available: https://arxiv.org/abs/1903.04584.

Chapter 7

# Token Generation Using Blockchain Technology

**Mahesh Kumar**[*]
**Poras Khaterpal**
**Rohit Kumar Mahato**
**Ayush Kumar**
**and Mohit Dayal**
Department of Information Technology,
Bharati Vidyapeeth College of Engineering, New Delhi, India

## Abstract

Token generation using blockchain technology is a revolutionary concept that leverages the power of distributed ledger systems to create digital tokens with various applications. These tokens are unique digital assets that, thanks to cryptographic principles, can stand for value, ownership, or even access privileges.

Blockchain is a rapidly growing decentralized network, which can be used for safer transactions. As blockchain offers immunity from hacking practices. To start, a smart contract must be created on a blockchain network that outlines the parameters of the token, such as its transferability, divisibility, and supply. Tokens can be generated, traded, and used for a variety of purposes after they are deployed. This technology has a big impact on a lot of different businesses, such supply chain management and banking. Proposed token can be used for payment, transaction from one wallet to another or token can be used as

---

[*] Corresponding Author's Email: malkanimahesh@gmail.com.

In: Blockchain and EHR
Editors: Kavita Saini, Amar Kumar and J. N. Singh
ISBN: 979-8-89113-380-8
© 2024 Nova Science Publishers, Inc.

an asset for the future like Bitcoin. Thereby the token is so important for decentralized transactions. Increased transparency, security, and efficiency are promised by token generation using blockchain technology, which offers a flexible and safe way to create and manage digital assets across a range of domains. In order to create and manage digital assets, token production depends on blockchain technology and makes use of Solidity, a programming language for smart contracts. This allows for the creation of safe, transparent, and programmable token-based ecosystems.

**Keywords:** token, mining, liquidity, blockchain, gas fee, bitcoin, Ethereum, fiat currency, crypto currency

## Introduction

Blockchain is a decentralized, immutable ledger that works by recording transactions done online and tracking the transaction assets done by the network. These blocks are "linked together using cryptography. Blockchain is a digital ledger where records cannot be retroactively changed without changing the consensus of all subsequent blocks and networks [1–3]. While digital twins are the complicated digital technology-based representation of resources that are rapidly adapted by industries all over the world, as a result of digitalization, some secure methods are needed to be developed for the sharing of the complicated assets of digital twins. Blockchain provides a solution to provide a secure transaction, and on blockchain, virtually the value of any purchase can be tracked [4]. We can trade on a blockchain network, reducing risk and cutting the overall cost of the assets. Blockchain is helpful in gathering information that is accurate and faster than normal processes like banking or any other asset. The information on the blockchain cannot be accessed by unauthorized parties. Authorization is necessary for accessing the information of a particular business and payments, accounts, orders, etc., can easily be tracked. Elements of blockchain, distributed technology, immutable records. Smart contracts can be used in monitoring supplies, digital IDs, processing payments and transferring money, data sharing, healthcare, copyright protection, IoT, and digital twin data. So, we can create a token system on blockchains like Ethereum and Bitcoin, gold, stocks, and individual tokens. In this chapter, we'll talk about creating tokens of our own. It will represent smart property as a secured token with no ties to conventional value.

# Token Generation Using Blockchain Technology

The key concept to understand is that the entire currency or token system is essentially a database with a single operation.

(i) If A has at least X units, subtract X units from A and transfer X units to B; and
(ii) the transaction has been approved by A.

All that is required to implement a token system is to implement this logic into a contract [5].

## Token

Tokens are crypto currencies just like real-life fiat currencies. A token can be used as a payment medium or as an asset. The value of a token will increase with usage in the market, and vice versa.

### *Mining*
Mining is the process of creating new coins or tokens. Adding liquidity is the pairing of two tokens (one of our own and the other an already-in-use token) together to decide the value of our crypto token. Gas Fee is the transaction fee charged by the blockchain for executing and storing activity.

Gas fee is calculated as:
Gas Fee = Gas limit * Gas Price Per Unit

Bitcoin and Ethereum are blockchain-based crypto currencies. These crypto currencies do not have a fixed value; their values change with the usage of these currencies in the market [6]. The greater the quantity these currencies are used in the market, the higher their value will be, and vice versa.

### *Fiat Currency*
Fiat Currency is the currency which has a fixed value. Fiat currencies are backed by the issuing government. Some of the Fiat currencies are Rupee, Dollar, Dinar, Euro and so on.

## Smart Contract

Smart contracts are the set of rules for the transfer of crypto credits between two artists. It is self - executive after deployed on the blockchain.

## Applications of Token

There are various applications of token. Table 1 shows a few of the applications.

**Table 1.** Applications of Token

| S.no. | Application | Explanation |
|---|---|---|
| 1 | This leads to cheaper and more efficient transitions. | One needs to pay an exchange fee for converting one currency to another; token exchanges provide a lesser gas fee and overhead for conversion. |
| 2 | The data will be open source. | All the data is open source for the public, and anyone can see transactions done, but it also requires a wallet address. Without a wallet address, we cannot track transactions. |
| 3 | Anonymous transactions | We don't need PAN cards, AADHAAR cards or any documents as verification for creating wallet |
| 4 | Data privacy | Our data is private on blockchain. |
| 5 | Can replace fiat currency | Fiat currency a limited boundaries but crypto has no boundaries |
| 6 | Charity | It could be used for charity |
| 7 | Institute and academy | Acceptance by institutes and academies for their transactions, payments, and other stuff. |
| 8 | Used as staking | Purchase it now and keep it until some time when its value increases. On December 31st, 2012, 1 Bitcoin cost *$13.45, which has* now increased to $16,603.67. |
| 9 | Has no border boundaries | Like fiat currency, it has no border, after which another currency is used. |

## Literature Survey

This chapter covers a detailed overview of the generation of tokens over the blockchain using smart contracts. To create a token, we first need to write smart contracts using Solidity programming language. The smart contract will be based on some already-in-use crypto. In our presented work, we are using Binance. After the creation of our token, we need to add some liquidity to it. Once liquidity is added to our token, it will be available for use by the public [7]. This crypto token can be used for transfers currency and payments.

## Problem Statement

As we are well aware, blockchain has so many advantages, Using blockchain, we are going to design a token on blockchain similar to Ethereum and Safemoon.

In recent times, companies have switched from centralised data storage to decentralised systems with clear terms and conditions for data storage. Simirarly, payment systems, for big organizations, institutes, and other firms require faster and crystal-clear payment records keeping. Using blockchain technology, it is possible to design a system to track payments and other records to maintain the transparency of their records. Blockchain-based tokens could help us transfer verified data in different ways without showing our private information to other people or systems we are using.

## Objective

Blockchains are smart contracts that enable users to exchange tokens on the blockchain without showing any information. We can safely share or tokenize privately and anonymously. There are some blockchain tokens already in existence including Ethereum, Selenium, etc. We are going to introduce a token on the blockchain just like Safe Moon, with some customizations. The presented token will enable users to buy and sell tokens and trade on the blockchain. It will also help in tracing the transaction history using some string. In case the user forgot the string, the users' transaction can't be tracked.

So, it is fully private and safe to share data through the blockchain platform. In this chapter, an overview and conceptual framework of token designs and management methods is discussed. Tokens are built with some features like wallet tokens, transaction views, and user interface views. Further, it is important to understand that the token can be used as an asset and exchange currency from one token to another at the same time [8].

The main objective of the preseted work is to lower the barriers of learning, research, prototype designing, and integration of token-related standards and protocols by allowing researchers to understand both on-chain and off-chain constructs.

## Methodology

Blockchain allows transactions without involvement of third parties like wallets, banks, and other applications. Tokens on blockchains are very similar to coins; these are smart contracts. Coins are similar to tokens, but they are different because they use a blockchain similar to that of Bitcoin. Bitcoin and Ethereum are coins, but as explained earlier, projects built on Ethereum can have different ecosystems and tokens than Ethereum's native token, ETH. Units of value issued in the form of digital assets by these projects are called tokens. Token development is a more commode complexes than cryptocurrency development. Unlike cryptocurrency development, token development involves building an entire blockchain from scratch using advanced programming languages. The blockchain developer who develops the coin is the core developer, and the crypto token development process is highly specialised.

### Creating a Contract for the Token

To create a token, we need the presets ERC20 and ERC20PresetMinterPauser. Preconfigured to enable token creation (creation), stop all token transfers (pause), and allow the owner to burn tokens (destroy). Contracts use "Access Control" to control access to the create and suspend functions [9]. The account that provides the contract is granted through the Minter and Pauser roles and are the default admin role [9].

# Token Generation Using Blockchain Technology 115

## Creating a Supply Chain

Write a smart contract (a piece of code), which will run on the blockchain [10]. For our token generation, we'll use Ethereum. An example of token generation is:

Once token is created, the next step is to create a supply chain. We'll now create the supply chain for the token. For instance, we'll create a token with a fixed supply of 1000.

```
Contract PXTFixSupply is PXT {
    constructor () public {
    totalSupply += 1000000;
    balances[msg.sender] += 1000000;
    }
}
```

## *Rewarding the Miners*

Rewards for miners mean providing some crypto value to the miner as an honour for the internal _mint function is a key building block that allows you to write ERC20 extensions that implement the unfolding mechanism.

```
contract ERC20FixedSupply is ERC20
{
    constructor () public ERC20("Fixed", "FIX")
{
    _mint (msg.sender, 1000);
    }
}
```

A token reward for miners is produced through the token reward for miners. The Solidity language one can access the current block's miner's address.

When someone calls the mintMinerReward() function with our token, a token reward will be created at this address. It's worth analysing and experimenting with.

## *Modularizing the Mechanism*

The contract already contains a provisioning mechanism called ERC20PresetMinterPauser. This is a general mechanism for assigning the

Minter role to a set of accounts and giving them permission to call Mint functions, which are external versions of Mint.

This can be used for centralised minting, where an external account (i.e., someone with a cryptographic key pair) decides for whom and how much to give. There are some very legitimate use cases for this mechanism: B.

## Analysis

The token is based on Binance Coin, which has a graph value of adding liquidity to the token required a gas fee of 0.00183589 tBNB for *10,000* PXT (see Figure 1 and Table 2).

**Figure 1.** Analysis.

**Table 2.** Amount and Gas Fee

| Amount | Gas Fee |
|---|---|
| 10,000 PXT | 0.00183589tBNB |

As a reference of how big crypto is, please see Table 3 [10]. There are so many crypto currencies available in the market, like Dogecoin, Ethereum,

Coin, Cardano, etc. It becomes an overwhelming experience to start token generation for the crypto market [11].

**Table 3.** Crypto Market

| Crypto-Currency | Market Capital (in Billion) |
|---|---|
| Bitcoin (BTC) | 846 |
| Tether (USDT) | 79 |
| Binance Coin (BNB) | 68 |
| XRP (XRP) | 37 |
| Terra (LUNA) | 34 |
| Cardano | 33 |
| Solana (SOL) | 33 |
| Polkadot (DOT) | 22 |
| Litecoin (LTC) | 9 |

## Transaction

When a token from one wallet is transferred to the wallet of another person it referred tried to as transaction. Transactions are fully secure on blockchain platforms because of the immutable property of this technology and hence hacking is next to impossible [11].

## Result

The work presented in this chapter results in the making of tokens. The transfer and exchange between currencies is also possible as explained in previous sections. Afterwards, it could be used to make anonymous payments to anyone. Tokens' value will also increase with time as the number of users increases.

## Future Scope

When the token is being created. We are now eligible to sell or buy anything with our token, even though we can send money to other users. One can purchase the token and keep it to grow its value. So, it could be taken as an asset for future use. Using Crypto for daily transactions will also lead to a more efficient and cheaper currency management system. Some of the future scopes of the token are:

- Acceptance by Institutional: which leads to data imputation so that no one can change out data/records.
- Implications of token payments by major retailers
- Can be implemented on E-commerce platforms
- In future is can be used for transaction in institutions, academies, healthcare, business and E-Commerce.

## Conclusion

This chapter has implemented token generation using blockchain technology. Tokens have a smart contract that is written in the Binance Coin. The proposed token can be used for smooth, fast, and secure transactions and can be either purchased or mined by miners. Tokens get their value when we add liquidity to them with already existing cryptocurrencies. After adding liquidity, the value fluctuates and totally depends on the amount of usage of the token in the market. The more it circulates in the market, the more value it will have, and vice versa. It has a much greater scope, and there are not many crypto currencies existing with a lower gas fee.

## References

[1] Ahmad S. S., Khan S., Kamal M. A. - *Current pharmaceutical design*, 2019.
[2] Vujičić, D., Jagodić, D. and Ranđić, S., 2018, March. Blockchain technology, bitcoin, and Ethereum: A brief overview. In 2018 17th international symposium infoteh-jahorina (infoteh) (pp. 1-6). *IEEE*.
[3] https://en.wikipedia.org/wiki/Blockchain.
[4] Singh, G. Ajmera and J. N. Singh, *"Data Analysis using ML on Geolocational Data,"* 2022 4th International Conference on Advances in Computing, Communication Control and Networking (ICAC3N), Greater Noida, India, 2022, pp. 6-10, doi: 10.1109/ICAC3N56670.2022.10074047.
[5] Gupta V., Singh J. N., Khan S. I. and Chabaque A., *"Blockchain-Based Electronic Voting System,"* 2022 4th International Conference on Advances in Computing,

Communication Control and Networking (ICAC3N), Greater Noida, India, 2022, pp. 2049-2053, doi: 10.1109/ICAC3N56670. 2022.10074384.
[6] https://101blockchains.com/future-of-cryptocurrency/.
[7] https://www.forbes.com/advisor/in/investing/cryptocurrency/top-10--cryptocurrencies/.
[8] https://www.bitcoin.com/get-started/how-bitcoin-transactions-work/.
[9] Narayanan, Neethu, K. P. Arjun, and Kavita Saini. *"A Blockchain technology for asset management in multinational operation."* Essential Enterprise Blockchain Technology and Applications (2021) : 153-178.
[10] Saini, Kavita, ed. *Blockchain and IoT Integration: Approaches and applications.* CRC Press, 2021.
[11] https://docs.openzeppelin.com/contracts/3.x/erc20-supply.

# About the Editors

Dr. Kavita Saini
Professor
School of Computing Science and Engineering
Galgotias University, Delhi NCR, India
E-Mail: kavitasaini_2000@yahoo.com

Kavita Saini (IEEE and ACM Member), is presently working as Professor, School of Computing Science and Engineering, Galgotias University, Delhi NCR, India. She received her PhD degree from Banasthali Vidyapeeth, Banasthali. She has 20 years of teaching and research experience supervising Masters and PhD scholars in emerging technologies.

She has published more than 100 research papers in national and international journals and conferences. She has published 18 authored books for UG and PG courses for a number of universities including MD University, Rothak, and Punjab Technical University, Jallandhar with National Publishers. Kavita Saini has edited more than 12 books with International Publishers including Elsevier, IET Publisher, IGI Global and CRC Press, NOVA Science Publisher and published 30 book chapters with International publishers. Under her guidance many M Tech and Ph D scholars are carrying out research work and few have completed under her guidance.

She has also published various patents. Kavita Saini has also delivered technical talks on Blockchain: An Emerging Technology, Web to Deep Web and other emerging Areas and Handled many Special Sessions in International Conferences and Special Issues in International Journals. Her research interests include Smart and Sustainable Agricultural, Blockchain Technology, Industry 5.O, and Cloud and Edge Computing, Digital Twin and Web Based Instructional Systems (WBIS).

About the Editors

**Amar Kumar**
General Manager, HCL Technologies Ltd. India
Mob. +91 9818523760
Emails (including business email): amark@hcl.com; amarkuma@gmail.com

Amar is General Manager at HCL Technologies, India. He is expert in Automation and Network security. Presently he is looking various projects for Network security and automation. He has done various certification including PMP. He is involved in writing various book chapters and in editing books. Amar Kumar has completed various certifications in his fields and has keep interest in working in the area of blockchain Technology, Digital Twin and various other emerging technologies. He is Editor of IET and CRC Press Books which are ongoing.

**Dr. J. N. Singh**
Designation: Professor, SCSE
Galgotias University, Greater Noida, India
singhjn2000@gmail.com

Dr. J. N. Singh is working as Professor in School of Computing Science & Engineering, Galgotias University, Greater Noida, India. He completed his master degree from Madan Mohan Malaviya University of Technology Gorakhpur and Ph.D. in Computer Science from BabaSaheb Bhimrao Ambedkar University Lucknow, India He has served as Chair in many conferences and affiliated as member of program committee of many conferences in India and abroad. He has supervised 3 PhD students and many M.Tech. students for their thesis. He published Number of research paper in Conferences and Journals and as a Book Chapters. His area of research interests includes information retrieval, image processing, networking, Software Reliability, etc. He is actively publishing in these areas.

# Index

## A

access control in blockchain, 89
advanced encryption standard (AES), 60
aggregation, 60
Alchemy, 77

## B

bitcoin, vii, 5, 6, 7, 9, 11, 14, 15, 17, 19, 20, 22, 25, 26, 37, 38, 43, 47, 51, 67, 75, 86, 94, 99, 100, 101, 102, 105, 110, 111, 112, 114, 117, 118, 119
blockchain, 1, 2, 3, 4, 5, 6, 7, 8, 9, 10, 11, 12, 13, 14, 15, 16, 17, 18, 19, 21, 22, 23, 24, 25, 26, 28, 29, 31, 32, 33, 34, 35, 36, 37, 38, 39, 40, 41, 42, 43, 44, 45, 46, 47, 48, 49, 50, 51, 52, 53, 54, 55, 56, 57, 60, 61, 67, 68, 69, 70, 71, 72, 73, 74, 75, 76, 77, 78, 79, 85, 86, 87, 89, 94, 95, 96, 97, 98, 99, 100, 101, 102, 103, 104, 105, 106, 107, 109, 110, 111, 112, 113, 114, 115, 117, 118, 119, 121, 122
blockchain approaches, 89, 104
blockchain challenges, 18, 22
blockchain network, 3, 4, 6, 13, 23, 40, 41, 53, 54, 87, 101, 109, 110
blockchain technology, vii, viii, 1, 2, 4, 5, 7, 8, 10, 13, 15, 17, 18, 21, 22, 24, 25, 31, 33, 34, 36, 37, 39, 43, 45, 47, 51, 56, 57, 70, 71, 72, 73, 85, 89, 96, 97, 98, 102, 109, 110, 113, 118, 119, 121
blockchain-based applications, vii, 33, 34

## C

cloud storage, viii, 60, 87
coinbase transaction, vii, 26, 30
consensus mechanism, 11, 18

ContentBased Identity (CID), 71, 74, 77, 79, 82, 85
copyright, 17, 110
crypto currency, 110
cryptocurrency attacks, 9
cryptography, viii, 12, 19, 33, 34, 43, 59, 60, 61, 67, 71, 76, 85, 93, 110
cryptosystem, 33, 34
Crystal Surveillance program, 37

## D

data privacy, 14, 22, 60, 69, 102
decentralization, vii, 1, 2, 3, 4, 5, 31, 37, 41, 47, 60
Decentralized Applications (DApps), 15, 16
designers, 40, 42, 49, 50
Distributed Denial of Service (DDoS) attacks (DDoS attack), 8, 9

## E

Early Health Information Systems (HIS), 81, 90, 92, 123
election process, 48, 51, 53, 100
Electronic Healthcare Records (EHRs), viii, 15, 89, 91, 94, 99
Electronic Medical Records (EMRs), 90, 92, 104
electronic voting systems, 46, 47
encryption, 19, 33, 34, 43, 48, 60, 71, 76, 85, 89, 93, 97, 100, 101, 103
Ether.js, 78
Ethereum, 1, 2, 5, 7, 16, 41, 49, 50, 51, 56, 57, 72, 74, 75, 77, 78, 87, 98, 99, 101, 110, 111, 113, 114, 115, 116, 118
E-Voting, 46, 51, 56, 57

# Index

## F

fiat currency, 110, 111, 112
financial, 2, 5, 14, 15, 24, 32, 35, 40, 47, 66, 76, 96

## G

Ganache, 49, 51
gas fee, 110, 111, 112, 116, 118
General Data Protection Regulation (GDPR), 63, 93, 96, 102, 105

## H

hash function, vii, 11, 12, 24, 28, 29, 33, 34, 47, 48, 76
health, 13, 14, 18, 35, 91, 92, 93, 97, 99, 100, 101, 102, 104, 105, 106
Health Insurance Portability and Accountability Act (HIPAA), 93, 97, 101, 102, 105
healthcare, vii, viii, 6, 13, 14, 37, 76, 89, 90, 91, 92, 93, 94, 95, 96, 97, 98, 99, 100, 101, 102, 103, 104, 105, 106, 107, 110, 118
hyper ledger innovative technologies, 46

## I

immutability, 1, 11, 16, 47, 101
Internet, viii, 24, 25, 31, 39, 47, 56, 59, 61, 62, 65, 66, 86, 87, 105
Internet of Things (IoT), viii, 19, 24, 32, 36, 37, 39, 43, 56, 57, 65, 106, 110, 119
Interplanetary File System (IPFS), 71, 72, 73, 74, 77, 79, 80, 81, 85, 87

## L

ledgers, 10, 11, 47
licensing, 17
liquidity, 110, 111, 113, 116, 118

## M

Man in The Middle Attack (MITM), 7
medical data sharing, 101, 102, 104, 105, 106
MetaMask, 49, 50, 53, 74, 77
mining, 12, 99, 104, 110, 111

## N

network speed, 11
Node.js, 78

## P

peer-to-peer (P2P), vii, 5, 10, 16, 25, 34, 38, 40, 59, 60, 69, 71, 72, 77, 101
permissioned blockchain approaches, 99
permissionless blockchain approaches, 98
Personal Health Records (PHR), 91, 93, 95
privacy, v, viii, 1, 7, 18, 19, 20, 21, 32, 43, 46, 57, 59, 65, 66, 67, 68, 69, 71, 85, 89, 90, 92, 93, 96, 97, 98, 99, 101, 102, 103, 104, 105, 106, 112
private blockchain, 5, 6, 34, 76, 106
Protected Health Information (PHI), 92, 93
Public Blockchains, 5

## R

React, 78
reliability, vii, 3, 123

## S

scalability, 6, 7, 51, 92
security, vii, viii, 1, 2, 3, 4, 6, 10, 11, 13, 14, 17, 18, 19, 20, 21, 22, 25, 35, 36, 39, 40, 41, 42, 43, 45, 46, 51, 52, 57, 59, 60, 61, 65, 66, 67, 71, 72, 76, 77, 79, 85, 86, 89, 90, 92, 93, 94, 96, 97, 102, 103, 104, 105, 110, 122
smart contracts, 1, 2, 7, 16, 18, 24, 50, 51, 53, 60, 77, 78, 79, 98, 101, 110, 113, 114

solidity, 16, 77, 110, 113, 115
storing data off-chain, 71
supply chain management, 14, 76, 109

## T

tamper proof data, 12
token, viii, 78, 80, 101, 109, 110, 111, 112, 113, 114, 115, 116, 117, 118
transparency, vii, viii, 1, 4, 6, 10, 13, 18, 45, 110, 113
Transport Layer Security (TLS), 93
Truffle, 49, 50, 51

## V

voters, 46, 47, 51, 52, 53, 54
voting system, viii, 37, 45, 46, 47, 51, 55, 57, 76, 107, 118

## W

Web 1.0, 64
Web 2.0, 64, 66, 67
Web 3.0, 65, 66, 67, 75, 76, 86
Web 4.0, 65
Web 5.0, 65
Web3, v, 49, 50, 59, 60, 71, 81, 86
Web3.js, 49, 50